Advance Praise for Sara Wiseman and
Messages from the Divine

"Sara Wiseman's latest books offers invaluable wisdom, insights, and advice for getting through the highs and lows of everyday life. It's also tightly packed with action-oriented exercises that are really powerful yet so easy and fun to achieve. This is my favorite of her many books yet, and I've loved them all!"

— **Debra Lynne Katz**, author of *You Are Psychic*, *Extraordinary Psychic*, and *Freeing the Genie Within*

"*Messages from the Divine* is a gem of a book, full of golden nuggets of divine wisdom. With her stories, exercises, and examples, Sara Wiseman has made the information eminently relevant and therefore natural in applying to one's own life. Truly a course in soul growth."

— **Servet Hasan**, award-winning author of *Life in Transition*

"Sara Wiseman unfolds universal petals of wisdom affirming over and over what is surely in every heart, what we all know to be true, yet what we ever need to be reminded of—how to open fully to this unfathomable gift of life. Thank you, Sara, for this beautiful book!"

— **Ajayan Borys**, author of *Effortless Mind*

"This beautiful book brings home the lessons which connect all of us to our souls. Savor each lesson as you walk this wondrous path with Sara and you will understand why you are here and the meaning of our journeys."

— **Debra** *...ath*

"*Messages from the Divine* is a compassionate and expansive guidebook for personal growth and evolving consciousness. Each message lovingly beckons us to remember, awaken, and to dive deeply into the experience of living conscious, empowered, and divine lives."

—**Danielle Rama Hoffman**, author of *The Tablets of Light* and *The Council of Light*

"*Messages from the Divine* is not just words on a page, but rather a transmission that helps us evolve into our true nature. When we allow the words to deeply penetrate through the façade of the false self, it creates an opening into Essence where everything we want resides. There is no shortcut to this place but there is indeed a pathway laid out before us in this instrumental and potentially life-changing book. Apply this simple and profound wisdom and watch your world effortlessly change."

—**Jenai Lane**, founder of Spirit Coach® Training and author of *Spirit Led Instead*

"*Messages from the Divine* provides a refreshing, openhearted approach to trusting in the Universe and its divine guidance."

—**Jodi Livon**, author of *The Happy Medium*® book series

"*Messages from the Divine* is written with perceptive and unreserved prose. Throughout, there are moments in which you experience your own soul and are reminded of the reasons that you're here. With truth and compassion, Sara gives us permission to embrace our imperfections and Divine inner light. You will want to keep your journal in hand!"

— **Angela N. Holton**, international coach and speaker, founder of Love Sanctuary

Messages from the Divine

Messages from the Divine

Wisdom for the Seeker's Soul

Sara Wiseman

ATRIA BOOKS
New York London Toronto Sydney New Delhi

BEYOND WORDS
Hillsboro, Oregon

ATRIA
BOOKS

An Imprint of Simon & Schuster, Inc.
1230 Avenue of the Americas
New York, NY 10020

BEYOND WORDS

20827 N.W. Cornell Road, Suite 500
Hillsboro, Oregon 97124-9808
503-531-8700/503-531-8773 fax
www.beyondword.com

Managing editor: Lindsay S. Easterbrooks-Brown
Editor: Emily Han
Copyeditor: Jenefer Angell
Proofreader: Michelle Blair
Design: Sara E. Blum
Composition: William H. Brunson Typography Services

First Beyond Words/Atria Paperback edition May 2018

ATRIA PAPERBACK and colophon are trademarks of Simon & Schuster, Inc.
BEYOND WORDS PUBLISHING and colophon are registered trademarks of Beyond Words Publishing. Beyond Words is an imprint of Simon & Schuster, Inc.

For more information about special discounts for bulk purchases, please contact Simon & Schuster Special Sales at 1-866-506-1949 or business@simonandschuster.com.

The Simon & Schuster Speakers Bureau can bring authors to your live event. For more information or to book an event, contact the Simon & Schuster Speakers Bureau at 1-866-248-3049 or visit our website at www.simonspeakers.com.

Manufactured in the United States of America

10 9 8 7 6 5 4 3 2 1

Library of Congress Cataloging-in-Publication Data:

Names: Wiseman, Sara,
Title: Messages from the divine : wisdom for the seeker's soul / Sara Wiseman.
Description: First Beyond Words/Atria Paperback edition. | Hillsboro, Oregon
   : Beyond Words, 2018. |
Identifiers: LCCN 2017054271 (print) | LCCN 2018005159 (ebook) |
 ISBN   9781501188282 (eBook) | ISBN 9781582706665 (pbk.)
Subjects: LCSH: Spirituality. | Life. | Consciousness—Miscellanea.
Classification: LCC BL624 (ebook) | LCC BL624 .W59 2018 (print) | DDC
   204/.4—dc23
LC record available at https://lccn.loc.gov/2017054271

The corporate mission of Beyond Words Publishing, Inc.: *Inspire to Integrity*

Contents

Contents

Contents

Contents

Preface

For much of our lives, many of us live asleep.

Yet there comes a day, early to a life or late, when we wake up. This happens to everyone, at one point or another.

The door simply swings open and we are invited beyond.

In this moment of awakening, all distraction and drama falls away and we experience pure beingness, a moment of awareness so exquisite and full that our hearts burst open.

In this moment we understand our true selves: Divine beings who are One with everything, all the time. No separation possible.

And from the moment we taste this nectar, this moment of pure Light? Our hearts yearn for more.

This path of consciousness, of freedom, of living from your soul, may well go against everything you've ever been taught by society, culture, your family, all of it.

And yet . . . it's the only path worth taking.

The secret to awakening? It's remembering who we really are.

Introduction

We often think we're different from each other.

Yet I have not found this to be so.

I've been teaching spiritual and intuitive awakening for many years now, and in working with so many different people from all over the world—folks of all ages, races, and genders, hailing from entirely different cultures and backgrounds, with different experiences and different ways of being—I have found that we are the same.

We are the same, because we are souls.

Outer differences aside, our inner struggle—our soul struggle—is the same: "How can I live as my true self?" or "What is my life's path?" or "What is my life's purpose?" or sometimes even "Who am I?"

Some folks I work with are in their twenties or thirties, just beginning to walk their soul path in this world. Others are at midlife: people who, even after decades of living, are still struggling to become their true selves. Others are older, yet still growing into the understanding of who they really are. This is because no matter where we find ourselves in our passage through life, all of us—myself included—are on a journey to awakening: a path that leads us to live as authentic, original, creative, and conscious beings, free from the shackles of Misbeliefs, the wounds of the past, and the tyranny of our own minds.

And when we do finally wake up to who we really are?

This is when miracles happen:

We step into our truest way of being.

We create lives that are original, inspiring, unique.

We walk bravely in the mystery.

We learn to love.

We awaken to a magical and mystical life.

We let go of the illusion of control—and allow the Universe to lead.

This awakening to yourself as soul can happen to any of us, anytime. It may happen in an instant, or it can take a lifetime. And when it does, we are invited into a new way of living: infinite, expanding, and free.

This book is designed to guide and encourage anyone who is ready to dive deeply into what it means to live as a Divine human—to move from a distracted, stressed, chaotic, and unfulfilling life to an authentic, joyous, and profoundly meaningful way of being in this world.

About the Lessons

The Lessons in this book are spiritual teachings that I received in meditation—they are messages from the Divine.

Receiving, or what some call channeling, is a mysterious process. It came to me unexpectedly, starting with a near-death experience in 2000 that instantly transformed my understanding. Within just a few minutes I experienced the radiance of Divine/God/One/All/Universe/Source, and this changed me—and my life—forever.

I sometimes talk about spiritual awakening as a door that swings one way: once you've gone through it, you cannot go back. This was how it was for me. After this experience everything shifted, and it became clear that my life, and my life's work, was to be a journey on the spiritual path.

In 2004, after many spiritual and intuitive experiences, I began receiving spiritual teachings in meditation. More precisely, I received spiritual teachings in writing, while in meditative trance.

The experience of receiving is always a surprise. Even now, I never know when it will happen or what I will receive. I've been awakened for months during the wee hours before dawn, and called to write in the dark while the house sleeps. I've had entire summers where I sat in trance, eyes closed, typing on my computer keyboard, as the words flowed through me without knowing what I was typing.

So far, I've had four significant experiences of receiving. The first was "The 33 Lessons" published in my book *Writing the Divine*. The second was *The Four Passages of the Heart* published under the same name. The third is yet unpublished, and the fourth is the teachings contained in this book. Each receiving has built upon the last, creating a progressive spiritual thought system, a new way of understanding our experiences as Divine beings in human containers.

People often want to know what guides I receive from. When I first started receiving, I did sense specific guides providing information. As the receiving continued over the years, the process became different. Now, I simply enter a meditative state, move myself—my mind and ego and personality—aside, and I become the scribe. There is no other personality involved at this stage—not even mine. It is simply the words flowing from meditative space onto the page.

When I first began to receive, I didn't understand what was happening—I was new to the spiritual life, just beginning to be conscious. Now, after so many immersions with the Divine, through the acts of receiving and reading and teaching these messages, I have become more aware. I believe that anyone who reads these teachings—which are not mine by any means, but rather received through me as messages from a loving Universe—will also have this experience of increased spiritual and personal awareness.

How to Use This Book

Messages from the Divine is a course in soul growth, designed with a progressive curriculum. You might try reading the Lessons and doing the Exercises start to finish in an orderly way, a little bit each day. Not a start-to-finish person? That's okay, too. You can also use this book as a divining tool: simply open it up to any page that calls you and glean the understanding that is there for you that day. The Universe will most certainly guide you to the teachings you need to experience tremendous shifts in your understanding.

The Lessons are designed to help guide you toward awakening in your own life, at your pace. Some of the Lessons might make more sense to you, while others don't at all. This is normal, so don't worry if it happens. As you continue to read and reflect—and simply go about your life—your understanding will open up. It is also normal to read a Lesson one day with a particular understanding and to reread the same Lesson later and have a much deeper understanding. The teachings work on multiple levels and will meet you where you are.

I believe everything happens in Divine timing. So, while there are some who promote a slam-dunk, blast-through-it approach to spiritual and personal change, I prefer to tread gently and honor the concept of readiness. Sometimes we're ready to jump into our true selves right away and sometimes we're just dipping our toe in the water. In other words, it's important not to force or rush soul growth. Often, the most important thing that can happen isn't anything showy or dramatic, but as simple as an internal "aha!" or emotion. Whether you have lots of healing and transformation to do, or if you've done a great deal of inner work already, be patient with yourself. Everything happens in right timing—especially soul growth.

The Exercises at the end of the Lessons are intended to help anchor the teachings. If you're doing these Exercises as a course of study, you may find it useful to keep a soul journal to write down your thoughts, feelings, and impressions as you work.

You'll find that the Exercises aren't particularly complicated. They may be as simple as a brief meditation, recalling a memory, writing in your soul journal, or even noticing something. They don't take more than a few minutes to complete. Why so short? Why so simple? Because a little bit of the Divine goes a long way. Every time you connect in—even if all you are doing is closing your eyes and breathing—you experience direct connection with the Universe.

As you do this work, a little bit each day, you will notice things start to change. Of course, you will change as your awareness expands, but your relationships, your path and purpose, your abundance, your health, your intuition, your creativity—all of these will also transform.

Even the stuff you thought couldn't be shifted—those big problems you thought impossible to budge—even these will start to move because you're more often living from your soul instead of mind/ego/personality and the Universe recognizes and responds to this. You'll find yourself speaking the language of the Universe, understanding the direct connection that happens when you are both relaxed and paying attention. You'll notice the Universe communicating with you: not only in signs and synchronicities, but with a clear, two-way understanding that you can use to guide your life. And most importantly, you'll find yourself living more and more often in Flow: that wondrous state where you let go of all need to control and simply allow the Universe to lead you to your highest possibility—easily, effortlessly, and in joy.

No matter what your background, what culture or group or race or gender or age you identify with, a part of you knows you're something bigger than your identity, your mind, your personality—the "you" that others say you are.

You're a soul.

And when you begin to remember who you really are, when you begin to live from soul perspective, you will find that everything shifts around you, as your life begins to expand in meaning and joy.

It's really that simple. And you can start right now.

Book I

Living from Your Soul

PART ONE

The Portal Opens

New Soul

What happens when a new soul decides to come in? When the baby spirit that's been floating around for months, or even years, is finally given the green light?

They say that some souls reincarnate immediately, taking on human form again, to continue their path and their lesson. Others hang out in the cosmos for a while, reviewing what they did last lifetime around, deciding what they want to do next.

Not everybody comes back as human, every time. Some religions teach this as karma. Maybe not everyone comes back to earth every time either. We cannot know this, but it must be so. Surely there are more ways to live as a conscious soul than as just a human body on earth? Some say we are from stardust, others from evolution, and others from a friendly stork who drops babies off at midnight. Many say we choose the family into which we're born: the mother and father who will raise us well or poorly, who will stand by us or abandon us, from whom we'll inherit the best or the worst of bodies, brains, and traits.

This one has a musical ability.

This one has a problem with drugs.

This one has a gift with animals.

This one has a temper.

This one can make anything with her hands.

This one struggles with reading.

This one is quiet.

This one cannot be without an audience.

In the moment in which our souls are conceived as new earth beings, all these things are decided. The mother might shudder with the knowing that something has shifted.

I am no longer alone.

Something is different.

Something else is here.

It's a very long voyage from the first possibility to a baby's birth. Many things can, and do, go wrong. And when a baby is born, we don't know what to expect. Has this new soul reincarnated quickly? Is this actually Grandma Josephine come back three days after her death, to be with her family again? Is this another ancestor, returning a few generations later, to rejoin the lineage? Does this child come from somewhere else entirely, so that we may never understand her? Has this new soul been hanging out on stardust and moonbeams, talking with the angels about what he learned last lifetime, and given a new checklist for this one?

We don't know, we don't know, we don't know.

It's all mystery, this new soul, this swaddling of blanket wrapped into a bundle that we can hold for the first time in our arms.

The gift is a mystery; the mystery is a gift. Consider the mystery of your own lifetime: who you once were, and what you will become.

Welcome to This Lifetime

The day of your birth, the portal opened.

One final push, and you were here.

Cold air.
Flash of light.
And that surprising sound, which you would later realize was your own first cry.

A harsh entry indeed, and then something that made it all worthwhile: the immediate enveloping of skin on skin, and you nested into her, become One once again, but this time from the outside of her body.

And there was something else, an overwhelming energy in the room:

The sense of love.

The sense of awe.
Hearts cracking open, expanding beyond wonder.

Hush.
The new babe is here.

Hush.
The new soul has arrived.

There is joy here, and magic.
For this one . . . this one! . . . is special.

This was you.

Blessed.
Sacred.
Arriving in a holy moment.

Even then, you might have remembered your existence here, and by this we mean this side, the etheric realm, quite clearly. Many efforts were made to instruct you on the process—explanations of how you would move through the portal in hopes that you would remember!

During your time in the womb, you could still connect to this side. You were spirit mostly, ever so lightly attaching to human form.

But when you emerged through the portal, your earth self attached to you fully.

It was a shock, indeed, as spirit left spirit and found itself tethered fully into human body, the new umbilical of soul to self. . . . And there were other shocks: the hunger. That surprising sound again, your crying. The absolute frustration you felt, at not being able to communicate as you once did, and then not being able to remember how to communicate, and over time, not remembering anything you once knew. . . .

You were, in essence, abandoned when you entered the world.

In fact, all of you were abandoned: untethered from your soul connection, without the remembrance of your true life in spirit.

Seven billion souls who can't remember who they really are!

Now, you must learn it all from the beginning. You must learn it every time you arrive! It's a process that happens over and over again, each time starting at the beginning.

And as for when you remember who you truly are?

Some remember early.

Some remember late.

But everyone always does, at one point or another.

Don't worry.

You'll start remembering again.

It's part of the process of soul growth.

To forget it all . . . and then to learn it all again.

Enjoy the journey

Slip back to a memory of when you were a baby. Perhaps you can remember a special toy, or a soft blanket. Or maybe you recall your mother's heartbeat, or someone singing, or the way light streamed into your room. Go back to this awareness, and recognize your soul. It sounds complicated, but it's not: this is who you are. You're just an infant, and you're pure awareness. You're quietly, calmly aware and alert. This consciousness you feel is how your soul feels. Stay with it. Let this soul recognition sink in.

You'll start remembering again. It's part of the process of soul growth.

LESSON 2

You Chose This

Many of you have been here many times before.

You . . . yes, you! You keep heading back to do it all over again, soaking in all the emotion and feeling and pain and love that happens every time.

You feel things differently here.

A few of you haven't done the journey as many times, but no worries. It's always the same:

You choose your experiences.
You choose your soul circle.
You choose the where and when.
You choose the personality.
You choose the human container.

There are so many variations in a human life! So many selections to be made. A unique selection of personality and human container. A unique selection of parent, family, early upbringing. And even when you select a challenging course—for many of you have mastered the simpler lessons—your destiny is chosen carefully.

It is discussed with you. You agree to it willingly.

You're interested in having this particular experience that you call "my life" because you want to see what will happen.

You're interested in having this particular experience that you call "my life" because you want to see what will happen.

How will you handle it?
What will you feel?
How will you overcome challenges?
Where will you fail?
What will you learn each day?
What will you learn in this lifetime?

It's all a grand experiment, isn't it?

All this showing up with nothing, not a dime in your pocket?
Just a helpless little baby, born naked into the world.
Enjoy the ride.

What is it that you really want? Even if your mind is confused or unsure, your soul knows your deepest longings. Working with your very first impressions—the very first thought or feeling that comes to mind, complete these sentences. Work quickly, and don't allow your mind to interfere. Let your soul answer:

What I chose in the past is. . . .

What I am choosing now is. . . .

More than anything, what I really want is. . . .

LESSON 3

You're Here to Learn

<hr/>

You're going to learn lots of stuff here.
But when we say learn, we don't mean things like math skills, or history facts, or any kind of specific knowledge.

Of course, we delight in those of you who learn specific skills in this lifetime, you who treat life as a feast of learning, always picking up something new to absorb and understand.

You can cook, you can care for a child, you can drive in snow. You can hammer, you can garden, you can tinker and fix.

This is a marvelous way to actively be in the world, taking each new challenge as a skill to be learned.

We also enjoy those of you who sink deeply into one subject for an entire lifetime: you write, or play music, or make art; you do a sport, you have a hobby, you explore one thing intensely, with passion.

As you may have suspected, those of you who are fascinated by one area of work have usually done this same work before: many times, in many previous lifetimes. Each time you come back you remember faster, you get to it earlier, and you have more fun creating!

Some of you will even come across the work you did before: You will read the writings you wrote! You will see the paintings that you painted! You will listen to the same music! You will learn the same surgery skills, or read the same scientific experiments! It is a case of you in this life finding the you-who-you-were in past life, linked by your common passion in one field.

Wherever you are, whether you are exploring everything all the time, or exploring a few things with great passion and intensity, the same thing is true: you are making good use of your time. You are actively striving to learn the curriculum.

In this wired world, this world of electronica, we see those of you who lock into that man-made hum, which is so engaging to the eyes and the ears and sometimes the mind. But that particular hum only leads back to the vibration of electronica. It does not tap into the sustaining vibration of the soul.

Dream even bigger than you have imagined possible. Then live it.

We say, experience more than this! The world as a teeming energetic Universe offers so much more!

We say, choose the broader curriculum. Learn what you don't know. Learn what interests you. Learn what's hard to master.

Your choices are limitless.

At no time will you stop your exploration of this soul experience, except perhaps the moment when you are in the portal, returning to spirit before you return again.

Explore until the last moment!
Explore until the last breath!

Be passionate. Be frantic with desire to learn in this way, even in proportion to your consciousness and your mortality. The closer you get to death, the more you understand the extraordinary experience of life.

We suggest you dream big—then expand that dream!
Dream even bigger than you have imagined possible.
Then live it.

It is indeed possible.
It is why you are here.

Recall a time when you were a child. You may find yourself filled with memories of being about eight to ten years old. Notice what you're doing in this memory: maybe you're involved in something that you love, maybe you're doing an activity, maybe you're focused on something. What are you doing in this memory? How do you feel? This is a clue to your gifts or talents. Are you using these gifts now? Would you like to?

You Choose Your Curriculum

Long before you arrived on earth for this lifetime, you considered what you wanted to learn.

All choices were available.

There was starting from zero, and there was starting from behind the starting line. Maybe you chose one of these positions.

There was starting from ahead of the starting line. Maybe you chose this.

In life, there is no right or wrong way for you.

Nothing is punishment, nothing is in favor of the gods.

Wherever you find yourself is what you have chosen, and if that path is a challenging one, we say, sometimes the most difficult lives are the most blessed. For it is in the most difficult circumstances—the beginning from well behind the starting line, the beginning with challenges and difficulties—that you have the opportunity to learn the most.

These are the true students: those who have dropped into their earth lives knowing full well that they have chosen the most challenging experiences. Experiences that will take every measure of themselves.

In these experiences, there is no other solution save waking up and getting conscious very fast. To remember quickly, from whence you have come. These difficult lifetimes may lead to early enlightenment, serenity, and peace. And yet, many of you find yourself taking a much easier course.

Why? Because of what you have chosen.

The easier path also has value. There is no need to rush. You may go faster in one lifetime, slower in another.

In some lifetimes consciousness may arrive early and carry you like a bright beacon. In other lifetimes consciousness may be only the faintest flicker; it may not arrive to you until your last moments before death.

Whatever curriculum you chose this time, none is better than the other.

Many souls on the planet choose the constant challenges of more basic needs, such as food and shelter. This is a very heady way to live, so close to mortality! Each day, each breath, uncertain, so that the living is alive!

Other souls choose experiences where basic needs are met, or even overly met; they live in excess, too much abundance. You would think that in these overly abundant lifetimes everything would be easy. But when basic needs are satisfied, other challenges show up.

> *Whatever curriculum you chose this time, none is better than the other.*

The curriculum of the personality is also a mighty lesson. The soul inhabits two containers: the human body is one container, the personality is another container—and often the soul and the personality do not get along! In this lesson, your challenge is not food or drink or shelter but rather wrestling these two aspects—soul and personality—so that soul is at the forefront. So that soul is the leader instead of the personality, the ego. For most of you this lesson will be lengthy, involving, and very challenging.

There is no easy way.
The door is narrow.
And yet . . . to walk through is the greatest joy!

In this lesson, you will lay down the outer expression (or the identity) of personality—yes, the part of you that you think makes you, you—lay it all down so the soul may lead. Yet this shrugging off, this letting go, this laying down and surrendering the earth personality to the soul—indeed, this is the greatest joy!

In this learning, you inhabit heaven on earth. Which, of course, is where heaven is anyway.

What are the situations in your life where your personality, your ego, is mostly in charge? Does this serve you or does it hold you back? When do you let your soul lead? What would happen if you "let go" of your personality? How do you think you would feel? How do you think your life would change?

Everyone Around You
Is Also in School

Do you see that man over there on the sidewalk, with his cardboard signs scrawled with "God bless" and "Anything will help"?

Do you see that woman in the luxury SUV idling next to him, not making eye contact?

Do you see that young man across the street, backpack slung on back, earbuds in ears?

Do you see that toddler being pushed in a stroller, mouth open in laughter, head swiveling at the delights of everything: sun, air, birds?

Do you see the woman pushing the stroller, overweight, dyed hair, smoking a cigarette as she pushes him?

All of these souls are here to learn, each with its own lesson!

And, we say, these are just the visible, present-time souls you notice, in your day-to-day lives. This is not even counting those souls who inhabit time and space, who you are not yet able to see or sense because they are in other dimensions. Just like you, all these souls have chosen their lesson plan before arriving into this lifetime.

All souls are in school.

We say, make no judgment on whose lessons are "hardest" and whose are "easiest."

You cannot know what the woman in the SUV experiences: her luxurious life also contains great suffering.

You cannot know what the woman smoking experiences: her downtrodden life also contains great joys.

Work your own lessons. Trust that others are busy with their own lesson plan.

Work your own lessons.
Trust that others are busy with their own lesson plan.
You do not have to be the same, or have the same.

You are here to learn what you came here to learn.

Focus on this task.

As you engage with the world today, hold the intention to fully notice every person who crosses your path. Look at each person directly in the eyes, or observe each person with compassion. Another way is to have a human interaction with each person: say hello, show kindness. Notice what happens, when you show up to others in this way, without separation.

LESSON 6

You Learn at the Pace You Can Handle

● ●

You learn at the pace you can handle.

Big changes in your life—the loss of a job, the passing of a loved one, an unexpected financial problem, a health issue, a crisis— all speed up your learning.

To have a near-death experience, in which you momentarily move beyond the veil and know the true reality of the soul? This expands you at an accelerated rate. In some cases, it takes you to consciousness immediately, so that you remember all that you have forgotten.

We say, you don't have to almost die to experience this; you can do it at any time. However, some of you, in your stubbornness or your fear, need a crisis of this magnitude to knock you momentarily through the veil.

You get to where you're so, so ready for an upshift in your learning. Yet because you're not going to do it on your own, the Universe steps in: all the collective forces that sense and know when a soul is ready to move to the next step or stage.

It's every little thing, this Oneness that you are part of and is part of you, that senses when you are ready to expand.

When you are resistant, rebellious, dragging your heels, hiding out, numbing out, skipping lessons . . . this is when the Universe will provide an experience that shifts you quickly, even instantaneously.

You may perceive these experiences as hardships. Yet the gifts of these lessons are manifold:

The gift of financial ruin teaches you that money is a false god.
The gift of social downfall teaches you that fame is fickle.
The gift of illness teaches you that the body is mortal.
The gift of an accident teaches you that everything changes.
The gift of betrayal teaches you discernment.
The gift of grief teaches you to enjoy Now.
The gift of failure teaches you fearlessness.
The gift of bottoming out teaches you to begin again.

You receive the lesson that you can handle. You are meant to grow! So when you are hiding out in a nonlearning, nongrowing, unconscious life, the Universe will seek to balance this.

You will be given a lesson that demands your full attention.

These lessons, which often involve letting go of a way of life or a way of thinking, are never punishments. They are meant to take you further, faster. You may kick and scream when you are first awoken, as anyone might do when they are roused abruptly from a deep sleep. You may wake up confused, cranky, angry, sullen. You may not understand why you are being woken up!

But as the experience continues, and as you begin to understand, you begin not only to learn the lesson, but to have gratitude for the lesson.

You begin to become free from the worry of money.

You begin to become free from the addiction of social climbing as you learn that we are all beautiful souls.

You begin to become free from the fear of illness, as you learn that we all inhabit human bodies, and we are all mortal.

You begin to become free from the worry of accidents, as you see that life can change at any moment.

You begin to become free from anger, as the feelings of adrenaline and drama and addictions give way to the desire for peace.

You begin to become free from the fear of being abandoned, as you begin to love yourself.

You begin to become free from the fear of death, for others or yourself, as you understand that there is no veil, there is no separation, and we are all eternal as souls.

You begin to become free from the idea of failing, as you begin to understand that failure is often the lesson that teaches you the very most.

You begin to become free from the idea of losing everything as you understand that grasping and clutching of things and ideas is all illusion; that being present to this moment at the highest, most luminous, most shimmering awareness, is all that there is.

> *Surrender to the true north of your soul.*
> *Trust that you are ready.*

You learn at the pace you can handle.

If you find yourself roused from slumber, rub your eyes and wake up.
Don't whine or cry or rage.
Surrender to the true north of your soul: the continued journey toward expansion, growth, love.

❧ ❧ ❧

Would you like to let go of the ideas of failure and shame? What holds you back? How do you think your life would change, if you released these ideas? When you connect to your soul's wisdom, what do you need to change in yourself, so that you can move toward this freedom?

Failure Is a Part of Your Experience

Failure is growing.

Soul growth always happens when you risk trying or experiencing something new.

It is true: many times, when you try a new thing, you fail.
You don't grasp the golden ring.
You lose the girl or guy.
You're a minute too late.
Nobody shows up.
This is to be celebrated!

Not for the failure, which is simply success not having happened yet. But because you tried something new, you extended yourself and expanded yourself to a new vision.

You moved yourself toward your soul's highest possibility in this lifetime. This is where all growth happens: in the willingness to risk, the willingness to try, and the willingness to engage.

You might think of a cocoon: how we can choose to stay shrouded, under wraps, hiding, numbed, asleep. Or, how we might emerge from our cocoon: showing up, being here, being humble to the fact that we may try and we may or may not succeed.

The trying is what matters.
The engaging is what is important.
The attention is where your soul grows.

And when you have faced failure once, twice, a thousand times in your life, something wonderful will eventually happen: you will lose your fear. And that is perhaps not just half the battle, but the whole battle for most of us in this lifetime.

No fear of failure.
No fear of loss.
No fear of shame.
No fear of death.

When you lose the fear of failure,
you are set free.

When you lose the fear of failure, you are set free.

This freedom may happen early; it may take you many years.
Or you may glimpse it in the last breath you take.
The choice of when is up to you.

But freedom finds us all, at one point or another. Anything you have suffered up until that point simply vanishes into true understanding.

When we begin to understand ourselves as the Divine beings we really are, we also understand our suffering in a new way. We understand suffering as experiences.

We let go of fear and begin to simply attend to the process at hand of living: of growing, expanding, understanding, deepening.

Thus, don't think of failure as an end, a block, a tragedy.

Consider failure as the way you will eventually become free.

Fail, fail, fail . . . fail again!

Each time look up and see "I am still here."
Each time look up and see "I am still worthy."
Each time look up and see "I am still soul."

Continue to fail . . . a million times!
But don't stay in the cocoon.

It's musty in there. Too warm, too wrapped up. You're dead in there, a shroud.
Break open into this life, and fail.

This is the path to freedom.

Take a moment and recall all your past "failures." Notice how the shame, anger, and disappointment surrounding these experiences come from your mind, ego, or personality. Now, notice what your soul is showing you about these same experiences. Do you see that your soul doesn't see failure at all? It sees unconditional love, acceptance, and a celebration of you on your path. Can you accept this view?

Skipping Ahead Is Encouraged

Once you have learned a lesson, you don't have to repeat it.

Once it's learned, you're free.

The learning of a lesson—such as standing up for yourself, respecting yourself, holding yourself most dear, loving yourself—often brings big changes.

A relationship may end.
A job may end.
You might move.
Your lifestyle may change.

Change will come, when you are learning lessons.

And it is this fear of change that tends to make you hang back in the back row, repeating and repeating the same thing:

You might attract relationships that are humiliating or abusive… and stay in them.

You might go to jobs that are dull and boring . . . and stay there.

You might live in places that don't resonate with you . . . and stay there.

You might have habits and addictions that keep you numb . . . and continue them.

You refuse to learn the lesson, because you are afraid of change. You repeat the lesson over and over, never learning it, because you are afraid of change.

And yet, of course, change is just how things are. Learn the lesson or don't learn the lesson. But there is no escaping change.

Relationships change.
Jobs change.
You will move.
You will live many different ways.

Even if you try to pull the cocoon around you more tightly, wrap the shroud deeply around you and hide your head in its suffocating warmth . . . change happens.

It is just the way.

You are here to live, not to hide.

And there is another part to this: instead of refusing to learn lessons, because you are afraid of what might come . . .

You might choose to learn lessons quickly, so that you can go faster.
You might choose to learn how to spot a lesson as it arrives to you.
You might choose to learn willingly, in trust that all is well.

Don't resist! Don't slink back in fear.
Learn, change, grow!

In this way, you will soon find yourself skipping ahead, to a different kind of reality.

You do not need to repeat kindergarten multiple times.
Learn the lesson, and then move forward.
Get in there, open yourself up, throw off the shroud, and let yourself learn.

Then, move on to the more interesting coursework of your soul.

The Universe will take you as fast and as far as you can go.
And you can go much farther than you even dreamed.

> *Move on to the more interesting coursework of your soul.*

If you want to be happy, let go of your need to repeat, repeat, repeat.
Let go of your need to resist, resist, resist.
Let go of your need to hide.

Instead, be brave.
See what needs to be learned . . . and learn it.

Allow what needs to change to change.

You can't stop it anyway.

This is an infinite process.

What's a soul lesson you've learned in the past three years? In the past ten? What's a soul lesson you're working on right now? Finally, what's the one soul lesson you hope to learn in this life-time? Do you think you will?

Chambray Shirt

Sometimes a certain type of clothing will bring you right into a memory.

A faded pair of Levi's.

A grey, hooded sweatshirt.

A pair of black Converse.

Styles of clothing so ubiquitous they've become a uniform for all ages.

A child might wear them.

A young adult might wear them.

An octogenarian might wear them.

And yet, there are other things that we find at the back of our closets, or that we spy on the racks of retro stores, that take us back.

Way back.

A particular piece of clothing can act as a portal into memory.

Whether we're wearing the outfit or just looking at it—even a photo can take us back to that time or place we once inhabited: our younger selves, our younger bodies, what we were doing in those younger years.

Recently, I was at an event with folks in their twenties and thirties. A young woman walked in, wearing thigh-high socks and a mini skirt, and for a moment I recalled myself back there: in my twenties, wearing that same outfit.

That same week, I browsed a vintage store and saw the exact Hawaiian shirt a friend used to wear.

And just a few days back, flipping through some old photos, I was stunned to find a picture of me and my father, departed now sixteen years. In it, I wore a faded chambray shirt and jeans, my hair about the same length as it is now, my glasses about the same style as now.

How things do come around!

My father has his arm around my neck, and my face is lifted up to the sun, and I'm grinning in pure happiness.

I have this shirt in my closet now. Not the same shirt. But a shirt I bought because it tugged on something in my heart, even though I couldn't remember at the time what that was.

I look at the photo and see my younger self there.

I look in the mirror and see my current self there.

I look in meditation and my future self beckons.

We're all wearing a chambray shirt: old me, new me, future me.

It's a portal, and it holds space for the past: all those memories of all that life. And it holds space now: this life, this Now.

We think we change so much, but the personality is cast at birth, or probably even before birth: we carry the essence of this personality, this body forward from past lives, even as we do the work of the soul.

We think we change so much, but looking back, do we change at all? The essence of soul carries us forward: the constants of body, personality remain.

The soul continues on and on and on—last lifetime, this lifetime, next lifetime . . . it is the only constant, and it is always expanding.

We live, we grow, we come around to see where we've been.

Will I still be wearing a chambray shirt at eighty?

I have a feeling it could be so.

PART TWO

We're Here for Soul Growth

School Run

I've driven kids to school tens of thousands of times.

My oldest is thirty-four, my youngest seventeen, with two in the middle. Which brings the tally of books and backpacks and lunches in paper sacks to a mind-boggling number.

If you've ever taken care of a child, you know: preschool, kindergarten, elementary school, middle school, high school . . . there are a lot of routes to a lot of places, with child and backpack and lunch in tow. There are a lot of hours at the sidelines of sporting events or in the audience at school programs, during which your heart leaps into your throat every time your child steps onto the stage of life—a soul-quickening every time you witness your child engage with the world, with all his or her confidence or fears or talents.

Over the years, as you go deeper into parenting, you log in more hours at school plays and programs and music and sporting events. You experience all aspects of their lives: dating, driving, job, graduation—the all-of-it that it all entails, and finally . . . after many years . . . you start to relax into the tension. You trust the Universe is with them.

You still want to protect them forever. But you know that you cannot.

You give them over to the Universe, and know that this is enough.

Nowadays, I only chauffeur one teen to school. We navigate twelve miles of twisting country roads each morning, passing through forests of fir and pine and maple, and meadows that change with the seasons. Many mornings, the sun is rising weakly in the east, fields streaming with streams, fog skirting the road. We drive carefully, for it's common to see deer picking their way across the road, flashes of brown and white. Osprey and hawk swoop and soar, and rabbits freeze motionless in the fields. Once a coyote stared at us boldly from the top of a hill, not a hint of cower to him.

When we get to school, everything changes.

The kids all look so free! Toting their backpacks, they walk in clusters of two or three, oblivious to everything around them. They're young, new to the world. We're still hanging on while they're pulling away, ready to walk their own path, to step out on the big stage with their whole self engaged . . . just as we once did.

I drop off my daughter and prepare for the solitary drive back into the country, where I'll write and work until it's time to pick her up again.

Love you!

Love you, too!

We are all souls on our path. It's exhilarating to be out in the world! It's thrilling to witness this happening for a soul you've known from a child!

Everyone around you is a soul. At a certain point, we have to let go of the need to control, change, or fix anyone else but ourselves. Souls can't do anything but fly free, have experiences, and learn lessons. Such is the nature of souls.

Be grateful, when you see a soul beginning to stretch its wings. Be amazed, when you see it start to fly.

Including yourself.

Everyone's Big Lessons Are the Same

Before you learn to remember, it all seems very complicated.

Everyone in the world who hasn't learned to remember yet is shouting at you that this is how it is, or that is how it needs to be, when the truth of the soul's lesson—and by soul we mean you—is simply to expand to the highest level it can reach.

As a human, you're limited by your personality, your body, and the particular time, place, culture, and surroundings you chose before birth.

Yes, again . . . you chose.

You chose this adventure.

You chose this experience knowing full well that it was going to be challenging, and that it would bring you to certain lessons: survival, security, stability.

Or maybe you chose this curriculum because those things were going to be easy: perhaps all the survival, security, and stability were taken care of in this lifetime. So you could move on to other lessons: love, consciousness, and understanding your infinite nature?

The question is, then, how far can you lift off from where you began?

If you've chosen a hard experience, what's the farthest you can go from there?
If you've chosen an easy experience, what's the farthest you can go from there?

We come back to earth, over and over, to see how far we can go.

We live, we die, we reincarnate, we live, we die. . . .
And in each new lifetime . . . we get to learn.
It's here on earth that we can expand, really learn our stuff.

We learn on the earth plane through our fear, our shame, our self-loathing, our pride, our judgment, our prejudice, our hatred, our anger, our bitterness, our sadness, our failure.

Each lesson of separation mastered helps us crack through to the fact that we're really souls . . . that our true experience, our true reality is eternal, unlimited and infinite. And when we get that, well, that's when things really start to change.

This idea that one day, we'll be able to live forever?

That we'll be immortal?

This is already true.

We're souls; infinite, perfect Universes within an infinite, perfect Universe.

We enter each lifetime to be human, to work on the same lesson that everyone else is here to work on, moving from separation to Oneness.

Do you believe in past lives? If so, do you remember any? Are there places, people, or activities you seem to just "know" even though you've never experienced them before? How does the idea that we're infinite beings change how you think about this life?

It's here on earth that we can expand, really learn our stuff.

We're Here to Find Love

In all your lifetimes, you're not going to learn anything bigger than this: we're here for love.

You may try to kick love away.
You may reject it when it shows up.
You may hate.
You may run away and hide when it gets too complicated.
You may live in fear and isolation, never letting another in.
You may think you're better than another.
You may think you're less than another.

All of these Misbeliefs are false.
Follow them, and you are simply led on a longer path to self-discovery.

Love between humans; love from humans to all the other energy beings on this planet: animals, plants, inanimate objects; love between humans and all etheric beings; love from all other

energy and etheric beings; love in time and space and matter;
love as a way of being that we learn to inhabit more and more
often, until one day, we just get it.

We just get that it's all love.

Love's the energy.
Love's the Universe.
Love's the particulate.
Love's the reason.
Love's the reality.

> *Love's a beautiful lesson. The biggest lesson there is.*

It's a beautiful lesson.
The biggest lesson there is.
And it may take you this lifetime,
and thousands more, to finally
learn it.

When you know it; when you really know, love cracks open
your heart and shatters through all the pain that you have held
in there so long.

This transformation, enlightenment, realization?

You'll get there, one day or another.

For now . . . simply notice love wherever it shows up in your
life. Follow it. Commit to it. Be in it. Thank it.

For now, just give and accept all the love you can, in all the
places it arrives. Your heart is expanding, even upon reading
these words.

How have you experienced love in this lifetime? Have you known love in romance, with a lover, partner, or spouse? Have you known love in friendship—either as a best friend or close friend, or even in a group of friends? Have you experienced love in family, in all the ways this can happen? Do you think you have it within you to love deeper, better, stronger? Do you think you have it within you to accept this kind of love from others?

We're Here to Have Purpose

* *

Each of us is given a particular soul contract to accomplish in a lifetime.

You may be sent here to write.

You may be sent here to teach.

You may be sent here to serve one particular soul or soul cluster, such as a family.

You may be sent here to sacrifice on a karmic level, for a soul you've been working with a long time.

You may be sent here to play, to enjoy, to experience.

You may be sent here to travel the world, or to live in specific places.

You may be sent here to heal others.

You may be sent here to heal yourself.

You may be sent here to build.

You may be sent here to stabilize.

You may be sent here to invent.

You may be sent here to inspire.

These are just a few of the ways your contract is written, but always there is one main trajectory, one main calling, one main purpose that is yours and yours alone.

Sometimes, we understand our purpose early: we get down to the business of living our lives clearly and at a young age. This is a marvelous gift, because in this way we have more time to focus on our path.

We have more time in the lifespan to give our full attention to our soul's calling.

But often, we waste much of our lives slinking and sliding around our purpose, wondering if it is really ours, wondering if we will have the courage to undertake this great calling in our lifetime, wondering if we dare to do it.

In these cases we become:

The writer who does not write.
The painter who does not paint.
The singer who does not sing.
The doctor who does not heal.
The explorer who does not explore.
The adventurer who does not adventure.
The parent who does not support a family.
The inventor who does not invent.
The motivator who does not inspire.

We forget to live our lives. Instead, shivering under blankets of fear and uncertainty, we hang on the edge of the diving board, refusing to dive in. We refuse to commit, we refuse to leap, we refuse to trust. We are living but we are not living our purpose, we are not living what we came here for.

It is a great waste, to not fully live in a lifetime.

Don't be afraid of what you don't know how to do. Just begin.

Trust that in the doing of the thing, you will learn all that you need to know. Don't be afraid if you will be a success by the world's terms. Success is not in any-one's contract.

Your calling is simply to do the thing, to have the experience, to understand the lessons that arrive from the doing.

> *It is a great waste, to not fully live in a lifetime.*

Don't wait until your life is perfect, until you have the time, until you have the space.

Begin writing at the kitchen table.
Clear out the garage and begin inventing.
Apply to school now.
Begin singing even as you walk to the bus stop.

When you are gone from this lifetime, when you are in review of this lifetime, you will see all the moments you were living from purpose, and how this focus, these activities, squeezed into place in the odd moment—the early morning, the lunch break, the afternoon downtime, the evening—created room for more living from purpose.

And you will see how all these moments spent moving in your purpose were brilliant gems, so much more valuable than the time wasted in addiction, in sloth, in must-do, in worry, in fear, in distraction.

Make room, make room.
Let go of what is not your purpose.
Make space, make time.
Begin to live your soul's contract, in every moment you are breathing.

And if you don't know your soul's contract?
We say, close your eyes. Breathe. Be still.
Listen, feel, sense, see. You have known your contract since your birth.

We say, it is the thing you are most afraid of, that excites you most deeply, that you most wish to do. It is the thing that if you were to start today, you would feel your heart expand in joy.

We say, you are here to live your calling.
If you still do not know your calling, we say, yes, you do.

Allow this.

Close your eyes. Relax. Allow your soul's purpose to arrive to you. Let go of the idea that you are confused, that you don't know. You have known your purpose, your soul's contract, since before you were born. Be still, and remember it now.

We're Here to Find Meaning

You want nothing to dissuade you. You want no distractions.

This is your soul's journey through this lifetime.

And yet, it is expected and known that you will become distracted by all that is in the bazaar! You will stop at the gambling tables. You will drink at the pub. You will waste time in disconnected sexual encounters. You will spend your money on trifles. You will look at trinkets and buy them, and then buy more. You will wander aimlessly, passing time, allowing each new thing to take you to the next and the next. You will get in arguments, overturn tables. You will be stolen from, and beaten.

You will do all these things, and more!

Yet at a certain point, you will look up and see the open sky. You will notice the clouds moving, curls and whispers of white against all that blue. And you will notice the shadow falling differently; and you will notice it is time to leave the bazaar with all its drama and distractions, and continue on your way.

You will learn this in time.

And you will understand that this lifetime is a container of time for you.

At the beginning of your soul's journey, you think that you can make every choice, have every experience, do everything all the time. Not only when you are young, but when you are older and insatiable for the "must-do," the schedule, the distraction, the drama.

Yet when you get to a certain place of understanding, you will realize that you are here for your particular lessons, your particular contract.

And that's the most important thing.

> *You are here for your particular lessons, your particular contract.*

You can't taste, see, experience, sample everything.
You're not supposed to.

You're here to find your meaning.

So don't dither and waste your time in entertainment, in numbness, while the journey still calls you. The shadows are falling differently already.

Get up. Begin what gives your life meaning.

Make a list of everything you do in a normal day, from the moment you wake up until the moment you fall asleep. Now, look at what is meaningful to you on this list, what truly expands your life. Let go of everything else. If you're not sure how to let go, ask the Universe for help.

Dreaming Is One Lesson

When you dream, you exist in etheric realms where everything you have forgotten lives.

Your set of instructions.
Your map.
Your soul contract, signed by you and copied in triplicate.
Your cheat sheet.

This place has many names, from many times and many religions.

And yet, there is no block to the door. You can go there anytime: close your eyes, breathe, ask entrance, and you are already there.

You have been here so many times!

Some of you see a garden with a stone bench.
Some of you see a building with white columns.
Some of you arrive in great white hallways.

Some of you arrive in a forest in which there is a small hut.
Some of you find yourself on a mountain vista with clouds below.

All these are common places for the guides to meet you, teach you, show you, and help you to remember your soul contract, your soul purpose.

> *Close your eyes, breathe, ask entrance, and you are already there.*

You cannot know these places, if you do not agree to go there.

We say again:

Close your eyes.
Breathe.
Ask to enter.

You will be in these places, and you will be with us, instantly.

You need no process, no special skill, no instruction. The path to God/Universe/One/All is simple.

You enter in upon the breath.
Try it now.
Try it today.
Go in, enter in, be in this place with us, where you can be taught, instructed, reminded, healed, comforted, enlightened.

And yes, some of you will see Jesus, Mary, Buddha, saints, and other Holy Ones.

Some of you will see angels, guides, etheric entities.
Some of you will see visions.
Some of you will understand.
Some of you will have your heart opened beyond what you thought was possible.
Some of you will know the nectar of bliss, joy, love.

The soul requires this refreshment, this nectar, this sweetness, this comfort, many times during the day.

To dream at night is not enough.

When you pray, when you meditate, do you allow yourself to see visions, to receive messages, to open your heart to everything? This is how the Universe speaks to us; this is the language it uses.

Being Is Another Lesson

When you dream you travel to the etheric realms.

You do this while you are sleeping, or in those states between waking and sleeping, sleeping and waking.

Yet there is another way to enter this place—this nirvana, this bliss, this nectar of pure consciousness.

Yes, you may go there by the more formal methods of meditation, trance, prayer.

Yes, these are marvelous vehicles.

But we say, you can also go there by simply being.

In the intentional act, in the putting away of doing and of thought, and simply existing in the "what is" of the moment.

Whenever you are fully involved, fully engaged in nothing, in No Thing . . .

This is your state of being.

Whenever you are free from thought of the next minute or hour or year, free from thought of the thing that happened minutes or hours or years ago . . .

. . . this is your state of being.

Whenever you are fully in your body, with no concern for anything else besides the joy of being alive in your body.

This is your state of being.

This being in Nowness, not in the past, not in the future—this is a marvelous thing! This being beyond time.

You might find these moments slipping upon you at the most unexpected moments: when you take quiet time on the sofa and sit in the room in peace, not reading, not on the computer, not talking, not writing. Just sitting, feeling your own body in the room, your own breath in your body.

Your body as particulate, in the soup and soul of all particulate.

Or perhaps you step outside for a moment and are stunned by the beauty of the sky above, the trees, the air on your skin. You stand in this appreciation and simply become One with all that is around you: a moment of being.

Or perhaps you are not alone, or not in nature. You are not still at all, but are right in the thick of life: riding on a bus or subway, driving in traffic, waiting in line at a store. And suddenly a sense of euphoria fills you, even in a situation where euphoria is hardly expected!

You can have a moment of pure beingness anywhere, at any time, whenever you stop all the doing and thought looping and past remembering and future thinking.
Let it all go.

Nothing is more important than being.
Being is all there is.

Stop for one moment.
Breathe.

Nothing is more important than being.
Being is all there is.

This moment. Fully present.
Next moment. Fully present.
And so on, and so on.

Put down this book. Put down your thoughts. Now, begin paying exquisite attention to everything. The air on your skin. The light around you. The euphoric presence of every little thing. Let yourself expand into this energy, this bliss. Hold nothing back.

Sing with Your Heart Open

I was lucky enough to go to Catholic school.

I know, it doesn't sound lucky to everyone, does it?

But for me, it was entrancing, exotic, completely different from life with my non-church-going family: the statue of Mary in the foyer, the weekly Mass in the hushed chapel, the fonts of holy water in every room, and the nuns garbed in grey, faces peeking out from wimples.

Sister MaryAnn, who taught us English and music, was my favorite. Unlike Sister Bernadette who was melancholy, or Sister Buena who was cranky, Sister MaryAnn exuded joy as she taught us to sing.

There wasn't a piano, there wasn't a choir room: we learned to sing in the same classroom where we did spelling and composition. The only difference was that we put our paper and pencils away and stood up, right beside our desks.

Sister MaryAnn worked out harmonies democratically, by dividing the room into quarters. This section of the room soprano, this section alto, this section tenor, and this section bass.

Girl? Boy? High voice? Low voice? It didn't matter to Sister MaryAnn. In her democratic system, you were called upon to be everything: soprano, alto, tenor, or bass. You sang whatever your section sang, whether this was your range or not.

And most importantly, you were required to sing *loud*.

That's because, for Sister MaryAnn, singing wasn't about the tone, or the range, or even the notes.

For Sister MaryAnn, singing was praying.

And if for some reason you weren't singing loud . . . if you were shy or mumbly or unsure that day, she'd march over to your desk and stand there as long as it took, hand keeping time like a metronome until, finally, in embarrassment or surrender or exultation, you belted your song out at the top of your lungs—full force, whole heart singing.

I always loved that she made us do that: open up fully, even when we were afraid, even when we didn't feel like it.

We always felt so much better after music.

Our hearts had opened, whether we wanted them to or not.

PART THREE

Being Is
the Way

Big Red Binder

Years ago, when I started teaching workshops, I always lugged along a big red binder. Inside was my cheat sheet, my security blanket, my salvation—outlines of my teaching notes, broken down into time segments and typed in oversized type so that I could read it from a distance without appearing to be referring to it at all.

I could not do a workshop without Big Red.

Even if I didn't end up referring to it, I needed to have it with me—tucked under my chair or on the lectern with me. I couldn't present without it.

Back then, a few things tended to happen when I was teaching to a crowd.

Often, I'd forget I was the teacher. I'd be musing over some concept I'd just heard someone say, then I'd realize that I was the one who'd just said it, and then I'd realize that everyone was staring at me waiting for further erudition. I was the teacher!

Or, I'd veer off into some time-space continuum where *time no longer acted as it should*, and hours turned to minutes, minutes to seconds. So even though I might begin a day-long workshop at 11:00 AM with great confidence and vigor, by 11:06, I'd have the overwhelming sense that I'd *taught my entire workshop* within those six minutes—and what on earth was I going to say next?

But the trickiest thing by far was that I'd lose myself in the souls of other people. I'd be teaching away, and suddenly, I'd have a complete recognition of one of the beautiful, amazing souls participating in the program, with such an overwhelming rush of knowing about this person, such compassion for this person's experience, that I'd get confused and lose my way.

At these times, I'd reach for Big Red.

I grabbed that binder like a traveler might consult a GPS, searching, looking, desperate for instruction. Where was I going? How on earth was I supposed to reach my destination, especially with all these other travelers depending on me to lead them?

Nowadays, I sometimes still forget I'm the teacher, and I invariably lose track of time. And even more frequently, I find myself gazing into the eyes of someone in the audience, and become nearly hypnotized by the beauty of that soul shining back out at me.

But I don't bring Big Red anymore.

I don't bring my notes because I've finally learned how to show up fully present, just get myself out of the way, and let the Divine pour through: teaching what the Universe tells me needs to be taught, facilitating what the Universe shows me needs to be facilitated.

When we focus on what we "should" be doing, we block what could be happening—awareness, flow, illumination, healing.

I never needed Big Red. All I ever needed to do was move aside and let the Universe work through me. Which I guess is the only thing anyone ever needs to do.

We Come In as Pure Being

When you were a baby, you lived in a state of pure consciousness, interrupted only by the needs of your body for food, warmth, comfort.

You did not need to be supplied with entertainment: everything was interesting, fascinating, a miracle. You did not need to be supplied with joy: everything was joy!

Even as an adult, with all your things and thoughts and mental constructs . . . you are no different than your infant self.

There is nothing more important than showing up fully in your life, and understanding that everything is fascinating, everything is a miracle.

There is nothing more important than your total immersion in everything!

And yet, you so easily distract yourself with everything that is not important.

By this we mean mental constructs, such as money or material possessions, and all the nothing that you create out of nothing: the dramas and anxieties and fears and rages that fragment your very essence.

We do not expect you to be able to lay your mental constructs down simply because we suggest that you do so.

We understand that it is only through moments of beingness, moments where you exist in a state of pure consciousness, that you begin to understand your true essence.

When you understand yourself as soul essence, so much of what you now see as important or even crucial . . . it all begins to drop away.

You come in as pure being: a babe, a pure consciousness.

There is nothing more important than your total immersion in everything!

You do not change as you get older.

We are here to help you remember, in this swirl of distractions that is earth life, the reality of your true nature.

Bring forth the memory of yourself as an infant. You might think you won't be able to remember, but you will. Close your eyes, and recall this younger self, when you had no thoughts, no language, just pure awareness.

So Much to Do, So Little Time!

On the one hand, you are eternal soul. And time is meaningless when you are infinite.

On the other hand, you're living in a human container. And for your human self, at least during this time on earth, the clock is ticking quickly.

You have seen this happen already: one moment you are young and fresh, the next moment the body has changed. You may pass a mirror, and find yourself staring at a person you do not recognize.

How has this happened so quickly?
How does the body soften and sag and falter?
How have so many years passed with so little accomplished?

We say, time is your friend, even as it is fleeting. The understanding that time marches toward death pushes you forward toward all the reasons you are here.

You may explore at twenty.
You may start a family at thirty.
You may write a novel at forty.
You may start a business at fifty.

You may move cross-country at sixty.
You may take up a language at seventy.
You may marry again at eighty.
You may learn to dance at ninety.

You may do these things or you may do different things: each of you has your own calling. But the point is this: time presses forward, and in doing so, time presses you forward.

The ticking clock urges you to use every moment, to hold every moment in your hand like the precious commodity it is.

Every moment you waste being numbed out, bored, disengaged, distracted, unhappy, enraged . . . you do not get this time back.

Time marches forward, to encourage you to march forward also: be in your life!

Not by busyness or "to-dos."
But by becoming fully engaged with every moment that arrives.

Fully here in this moment.
Fully here in the next moment.
Your whole life a beautiful string of pearls, an exquisite necklace of being.

And it's all yours for the creating!
All you have to do is say yes, and move forward.

How fully have you experienced this life? Have you done every-thing you wanted to? Have you experience all you longed for? If you have not, what holds you back now? If your answer is anything but nothing, ask yourself: is this really true?

*Your whole
life a beautiful
string of pearls,
an exquisite
necklace
of being.*

Learning to Be Is One of Our Biggest Lessons

There's this confusion about being.

In modern culture, we are told to forget about "doing" and concentrate on "being." As if we're supposed to be sitting around in our lives, locked in lotus position, doing nothing, no thing.

This is a misunderstanding.

We are not meant to slack, to waste life, to hang back, to not experience.

We are meant to have a life rich with a variety of experiences, so that we are continually expanding our understanding of our self in the world.

Being doesn't mean not doing.

> *We are not meant to slack, to waste life, to hang back, to not experience.*

It means not doing things mindlessly. Not doing things by rote, that are not well considered, that are old, that are of the past, that are not conscious, that are not who we are.

Often it means doing many things, as many as you like, but from a state of being, a state of consciousness, a state of wonder and awe and pain and grace:

So you do the dishes in mindful awe.
You go to a coffee shop in conscious connection.
You do your work in gratitude and service.
You show up to relationships with patience.
You do unpleasant tasks with compassion.
You laugh more than not.
You hold humorous and loving perspectives more than not.
You relax and take it easy, even when you are most active.
You show up fully, in a full state of being.

Do you see the difference? Between hiding out in false "being"— which is really just another way of pulling more armor around your heart—and really showing up fully? Fully present, fully engaged, fully here?

We say, show up either fully active or fully relaxed. And in each or either state, be fully engaged, solely focused on what you are doing and being at that moment, and then at that next moment, and then at that next moment.

Fully engaged. Fully present!

Whether you are full throttle or in peaceful repose.
Be fully engaged, in the human experience, in the soul experience.
Be fully present in both worlds, at all times.

This is the true meaning of just "be," of being in the Now.

Fully engaged! Fully present!

In all aspects of everything, all the time.

Is there a time in your life that you remember being fully present? What do you think it would be like to live at that level of engagement every day? How do you think your life would change, if you started to live this way?

Being Opens Up Everything

What happens when you are fully present, fully engaged? What happens when you are living continually from a state of "being?"

What happens is that you live from your soul.

You let your soul lead.

And by doing this, much, most, or maybe even all of your thought patterning—the looping into the past; the looping into the old story, the old wound, the old anger; the looping into the future; the fears and the worries of what might happen—all these patterns and projections, all these Misbeliefs and untruths . . . they simply dissolve and dissipate.

It is not possible to be in a state of full beingness and at the same time hold on to those old negative thought patterns, or even those future thought projections. The vibrational level you inhabit when you are "being" does not allow them.

It's as if they are sifted out, or dropped.

They can't coexist.

For example, perhaps you are experiencing a depressive moment. Then something comes into your life: a playful animal, a delightful child; or something funny comes into your view, or someone hugs you warmly and full of love, or you experience something absolutely miraculous and heart opening. . . . Any of these will jolt you out of your negative and depressive thought looping, and bring you instantaneously into a state of bliss and full beingness.

This shift causes you to forget the depressive or low-vibration state because when you are in a high-vibration state you see things from an entirely different perspective.

From soul perspective.

Soul perspective brings about states of full presence, interest, engagement, bliss, love, joy, gratitude, contentment, peace. Feelings that supersede any negative or low-vibration thought patterns.

The high vibration trumps the low vibration.
Levity always beats gravity.
We flow, as souls, to our highest possible vibration.

> *We flow, as souls, to our highest possible vibration.*

And, of course, the more you experience this high vibration of beingness, the more you want to be there. And, thus, the more you are there.

And so on and so on, spiraling up and expanding to our highest soul self.

It begins with being, with full presence and full engagement. The rest happens naturally, because it is our nature to rise.

When have you been in high vibration? When has your vibration been low? Do you believe you can choose your vibrational level, in any given moment? What happens if you raise your vibration, right now?

LESSON 19

The More You Can Be, the More You Enjoy

When you are fully present, you become exquisitely attuned to the "what is" of everything.

You know how it is when you are in nature, noticing everything, when suddenly the wind picks up and the leaves rustle in the air, and a chill goes down your spine because you are so fully there, so incredibly alive in that moment? And you realize that all the thoughts that you had in the moment before you noticed the wind and the leaves and your spine—the looping, distracted worries—were attaching your energy to old times, old places, old people?

You realize, in that moment of exquisite noticing, those thoughts simply vanish?

And you are fully present, fully alive, with simply what is: the wind, the leaves, the shiver down your spine.

And in this moment of absolute consciousness, exquisite noticing, exquisite sensitivity, you are flooded with feelings of bliss, peace, awe, and wonder.

This is what it feels like to be living from your soul!

So that every little thing—every little thing!—is worthy of holding your most rapt attention, for its beauty, and its profound perfection.

> *When you are fully present, you become exquisitely attuned to the "what is" of everything.*

Even the things that are not so beautiful: when you turn this rapt attention, this full soul presence to those things, through this lens, they are also beautiful.

The more you show up in your life with this full attention—letting go of the habits of thought looping, what is in the past, what may be in the future, and just showing up to what is—it is here that you begin to experience peace, contentment, joy. It is here that you begin to rest in the miracle of Nowness . . . this Nowness!

And you begin to understand that there is no place you would rather live, or be than right here, right now.

Regardless of situation, regardless of experience.

It's all amazing, when you exist from soul perspective.

Close your eyes and let all your thoughts crowd in. For a moment, let them swirl in chaos and confusion. Now, release each thought, as simply as if you were blowing dust from your open palm. Notice the calm presence that remains. This is your soul.

Break Room

Decades ago, when the building I worked in was one of the tallest and newest in Seattle, I was a file clerk for a big insurance company.

My sole duty was to push a metal cart around the office, stop at each of the many agent desks scattered in one enormous room, collect all the files stacked in their out boxes, and then slog back to file them in the dozens of metal filing cabinets that filled the back room, in alphabetical order.

Arthur comes before Atura.

McNab comes after Macnab.

Brighton comes before Broghten.

Calumus comes after Caluminus.

I became an expert alphabetizer, during the eight hours a day, five days a week I did this job.

The work days were all the same: the agents yakked on their phones and clattered on their typewriters and pounded their staplers and smoked up a storm of cigarettes. Back then, almost everyone smoked, everywhere.

Breaks were right on schedule: exactly three hours and fifty-nine minutes. The round, white clock on the wall would do that little clicking sound, and everyone would stand on cue and file out for their break.

Fifteen minutes.

Every four hours.

We punched out with a little card.

At that time everyone herded over to the break room with its metal chairs and one free landline, and proceeded to smoke as many cigarettes as they could in fifteen minutes.

I lasted about two breaks in that room, acrid with yellow smoke and depression, and then I started sneaking away; misfit, miscreant that I was, I hung back from the pack and rode the elevator down to the ground where I stepped outside and turned my face up into the Seattle rain.

I didn't last long at that job, expert alphabetizing skills notwithstanding.

I wish I could say that I quit, but I didn't: I needed the money too much. But I never went back to the break room, and soon after, I got laid off. Thank you, Universe.

It was decades ago. Those were different times.

But it's good to remember how silly we can be, how stunted, how numbed, how unaware. How someone might put up with something like sitting in a room smoking an entire break, an entire life away.

It's good to look back and see that we have made some progress.

PART FOUR

Everything Is a Miracle

Resurrection of Roses

I once worked as a photo stylist for a project that required thousands of dollars' worth of flowers: exotic roses flown in from Brazil.

The problem was, the shipment arrived late. The roses had been in transit for several days, and as I opened the boxes and pulled off layers of damp newspaper, I dreaded what I would find. Sure enough, the roses were severely dehydrated: crying out with thirst, leaves curled, petals singed.

I rushed to trim their stems and plunge them into cold water, as is protocol for reviving wilted flowers. But it wasn't enough. Even after thirty minutes, their heads were still drooping in that sad, drop-down way that shows they've given up.

I didn't know what to do. It seemed hopeless.

I was on my way to tell the photographer that the roses were unusable, that the shoot would have to be cancelled . . . when suddenly, my head filled with water: waterfalls, mountain streams, gigantic bathtubs with claw feet. Dripping, flooding, pooling water. Glacial lakes, icy fjords . . . the visions flooded my mind, and it occurred to me that I might hydrate the entire rose—not just the stem—but head and all.

I quickly plunged the first one into an icy bath, then the next and the next. I worked until they were all submerged, hundreds of flowers, and by the time I was done, I was covered in sweat and petals.

And then I watched as a miracle happened.

Within minutes, the dry leaves were unfurling, turning lush again, and the petals were plumping. Even the droopiest buds undrooped. These roses weren't just useable, they were perfect! They seemed to sing to me as I carried them, dripping water and beauty, into the studio.

So many times in my life, miracles have happened when I've least expected them. We think it's hopeless, we're stuck, and we can't go one step further on our own. And that's when it happens: when we finally surrender to a power greater than our own, we receive the answer, the guidance, and the exact solution for our next step.

It's the Universe talking to us, as it always does.

It's us listening, as we sometimes do.

Everyday Enlightenment

Here's this funny thing: when you start waking up, when you start becoming conscious . . . it's confusing.

You keep getting pulled back and forth between your regular self, with all those distractions and feelings and ups and downs, and your soul Self, which is beginning to show you how to live in bliss. You keep moving from regular life, again with all the drama and feelings that arrive there, and soul life, which is a steady infusion of pure love, peace, calm. So you're getting a taste of what's there . . . but you also keep getting yanked back into earth life.

This can be one of the most frustrating times, this passage where you can see the bliss, taste it, know it . . . and yet, you can't sustain it all the time.

And yet, little by little . . . over weeks, or months, or years, something begins to shift. You begin to taste bliss, nirvana, love, peace—whatever you want to call enlightenment—you begin to experience it more often.

And then, out of nowhere, on an ordinary day, everything suddenly becomes extraordinary.

You get out of bed, and instead of the normal crankiness as you move from sleep into moving about, you sip your cup of coffee or tea and you just feel . . . incredible. As if your whole Self has just become fully present and fully expanded.

You step into the shower and can't believe how amazing it is. You drive your kids to school aware how exquisitely beautiful this day is, this moment, as they chatter and laugh in the back seat.

You're at a work meeting, listening to information that isn't interesting or enjoyable to you, and suddenly you find yourself infused, washed, bathed in waves of happiness.

You find yourself soaring into bliss state, right in the middle of a work meeting!

You're doing the dishes after dinner, a task you don't usually enjoy, and out of nowhere, you are overcome by the sheer beauty of doing the dishes.

It makes no sense.
It makes all the sense in the world.

You stand there, doing the dishes, letting the waves of amazingness crash through you.

These moments of knowing the extraordinary within the ordinary . . . they start to happen more and more. They snowball. You begin to open, you begin to feel amazed, you begin to feel as if every little thing is connected, has meaning, is beautiful. And the more you allow yourself this feeling . . . the more you receive of this feeling.

Every moment becomes a miracle.
And you, fully present to this shift, get to experience it all.

Where are you on this path of moving from ordinary life to living from your soul? What do you need to release, in order to live in miracles and bliss? Fear? Anger? Pain? If you need help, ask the Universe to assist you now.

Every moment becomes a miracle.

Numbing Out Is a Waste of Time

This taste of bliss? This glimpse of Oneness?

It becomes the feeling you seek.

You realize that the drinking and drugs and food and porn and sex and shopping and gaming and internet and media and drama and overwork and over-achievement and busyness and fame and money and all the other obsessions and addictions you depend on to get you through the day. . . they no longer work.

Nothing compares to this soul sense.
Nothing compares to entering this bliss state, when you feel everything, every little thing.

So why do you choose to numb out?
Why do you choose to experience less than, rather than more?

Because of what you have been told, which is Misbelief.

That drinking and drugs and food and porn and shopping and gaming and internet and media and sex and drama and over-work and over-achievement and busyness and fame and money are all "good," or even perhaps that they are all "bad." And whether good or bad, these distractions are enjoyable. That they feel good. That they will make you happy. That you deserve them.

> *Why do you choose to experience less than, rather than more?*

Except, you know already: you can fill yourself to the brim with all the distractions in the world . . . and it won't make you happy. It can't. These are just temporary experiences that take you away from Now, as it really is. And the result is a cycle of pain:

You feel fantastic . . . but then you feel sad.
You feel amazing . . . but then you feel terrible.
You feel powerful . . . but then you feel like a loser.
You love yourself . . . and then you hate yourself.
You feel bigger than life . . . and then you wonder why you live.

This rise and fall cycle is characteristic of all of these: substances, habits, addictions, distractions, drama. It's all adrenaline rush, hormonal rush, emotional rush, brain rush, body rush.

And the up is tremendous. But the down? The down does not serve you.

And this is why numbing out doesn't work. Because it doesn't last. Because it doesn't move you from your reality. It just masks it, temporarily.

Whereas, if you choose to release yourself from all the numbing agents and stop distracting with them and, instead, just look at what really is, and be with what really is . . . then you have a chance to move forward, to expand, to move beyond this dismal cycle of pain.

To move from pain into joy.

And yet, of course, to get beyond the cycle of pain you have to break the cycle.

And at first this is difficult. At first, you do need to look at the pain, at all the pain you haven't looked at before, everything you've avoided, that has made you angry or afraid or sad.

So it is: Stay stuck and distracted, and keep returning to the pain over and over again. Or move forward.

No matter where you are in the cycle of pain–distraction–pain–distraction, it is always your choice.

Break the cycle, feel the pain fully. Feel the discomfort and all the feelings; sit with them and be with them. Until, one day, you will no longer feel the discomfort and you will be free.

What's your biggest addiction? When did it begin in your life, and what did you use it for then? Now, consider how your addiction is working in your life now. . . . Is it helping you? Is it really working for you? Or is it preventing you from growing past your pain, and being with what really is? How would your life change, if you released your need to numb out?

Distractions Are Not Worthy of You

•❖•

You are not here to distract yourself from your experience.

You're here to be in your experience.
This is the only way you can grow.

This includes experiences we consider enjoyable, meaningful, and "good." And also experiences we consider difficult, distasteful, and "bad."

It's not a moral view.
Everything is experience.
The view is what meaning we attach to it.

Thus, when you look at all the ways you think about your experience, don't judge it from a moral view, such as illness is "bad" or divorce is "bad" or drugs are "bad" or porn is "bad."

Or, conversely, that health is "good" and marriage is "good" and sobriety is "good" and purity is "good."

There is no use in labeling as "bad" or "good."

These are experiences only.
All experiences are chosen.

Everything is provided so that you may learn.
Not only in this lifetime, but in all the lifetimes you have and will inhabit.

Thus, the question is rather: Does the experience of drugs, drinking, porn, binge eating, and so on and so on make *you* feel better or worse?

The question is rather: Is this experience worthy of you?

> *The question is rather: Is this experience worthy of you?*

The question is rather: Is this the reality you prefer to create?

In other words: Of all the realities you can choose to create (and yes, you can create anything, *anything!*), is this the reality you prefer?

Yes, there might be an initial false euphoria with the drama/distraction/drug: the shattering of everything that makes us believe that we have transcended all our problems and are invincible and happy and satisfied at last!

And yes, there is also the inevitable aftermath, the contraction and despair when the addiction, distraction, binge is over ... when we have finished flying and feel terrible, awful, that we have descended into a dark hole of shame and unworthiness that it is impossible to climb out of, and that we are not enough.

Is this is your experience, is it worthy of you?

For, of course, you are enough. You are perfect, beautiful, whole Light. You are eternal soul. There is no reason to not understand and feel this in every moment.

And yet, a false, tempting, silky cycle of darkness makes you feel otherwise.

When you add dark to Light, it will hide or cover or damp down the Light.

When you add Light to dark, it illuminates, reveals, shows all.

In this way, you can see what you need to see.

When something continually takes you to a place of lower vibration, shame, unworthiness, sadness, pain, anger, despair ... this is not worthy of you.

Break the cycle, even once.
Look at what is.
Feel it all.

You will begin to see that you can move beyond distraction, addiction, numbing; you can expand beyond this reality.

You are an infinite soul, one with God/Universe/Divine/One/All. What happens when you allow yourself to remember who you really are? Close your eyes for a moment, and feel yourself as you truly are. Do you see how the craving for distraction drops away, the fascination with darkness leaves you? What would happen if you allowed yourself to live from this place, all the time?

The More Time You Spend Aware, the Better Your Life Gets

You can't drink poison and expect to be cured.
Poison only poisons.
This is what poison does.

You can't add dark to something and expect to see Light.
Darkness only adds more darkness.
This is just what it does.

When you are aware for even a moment, when you spend even a moment in consciousness, you begin to feel differently about everything.

About your life.
About your situation.
About your circumstance.
About your Self.

When you are in Divine space, there is no shame, anger, pain, despair. There is no need to numb yourself when you exist in this vast space of Light.

We say, this is how you can live all the time!
We say, this can be your experience always, if you choose.

It is simply a matter of leaning toward the Light, over and over again.

In every moment, you have this choice: darkness or Light.
In every moment, you can choose and you do choose.

It is always your choice.

We say also, you can choose dark your entire life: every moment, every opportunity, every chance. And then in one moment you can choose Light.

And this one choice will change everything.

Light illuminates dark.
Levity trumps gravity.
The soul rises from the mundane.

We say, attach to the essence of what you are: Light leaning toward more Light.

Understanding this, know this, be this!

Your reality is formed by your intention, by your attention, by what you choose.

When you choose Light, this becomes the place you exist.
This is a much more enjoyable way to live.
There is no contraction here, no shame or despair.

There is only love, joy, expansion, and further expansion, as you exist as your true unlimited Self.

In what aspects of your life are you being asked to lean to the Light? List them now, without shame or pain. Is there really a need for you to continue with these? Could it be that you're ready to be free?

> *Your reality is formed by your intention, by your attention, by what you choose.*

Pure Consciousness
Is 100 Percent

Being is the path.
Being is the reason.
Being is the way.

The result of being, of turning away from distraction and should and must-do and group thought and Misbelief and all the ways you hide from your life in fear . . . the result of being is pure joy.

It's nectar.
It's flow.
It's engagement.
It's connection.
It's expansion.
It's love.

Surely, these are ways you would like to feel? Not now and then, but all the time?

Being is the path. Being is the way.

You search for all false distractions, you believe what isn't real, you travel on false paths, you push and push and push against time . . .

. . . when all you have to do is be.

It's so easy.
You might say, it's so easy it's hard.
Seven billion souls who've forgotten who they are.

And when you do remember who you really are—that you are just here to be, to experience, to enjoy—it's then that you do remember how to drop into these states of being, of relaxation, of engagement, of purpose, of connection.

In these moments, in these ways of being, there are no seconds, minutes, hours.

Time stops—or expands, you might say.

We say, there is no time.

Thus, in these moments where you are fully in a state of being, you begin to inhabit consciousness differently. Each moment, if you can call it that, becomes 100 percent. You drop into the purest experience of infinite energy continuum.

It couldn't be stronger or better.
You couldn't get any more out of it.

It's not possible for it to be more.
It's 100 percent.

We say, it's possible to create a life that contains more and more of these moments. It's possible to create a life that contains more of these experiences of total engagement over and over again, without end.

In fact, you can create this without doing anything.

Because doing nothing—doing no thing—is exactly what is required.

You don't need more money.
You don't need more stuff.
You don't need a better car or house or clothes or whatever it is.
You don't need more friends.
You don't need a better body.

That's all outer shell, distraction, what you're told will make you happy.

When really, all you need is to learn how to be, just for one minute.

To drop into full engagement, to fully notice what's here right now.

And see how that feels.

You don't need to close your eyes, or sit a certain way, or say a mantra.

Just show up to what is.

For just one moment, drop out of human chaos and drama and distraction.

Let all your mind chatter go.

And look at this moment, this exact moment! from the perspective of your soul.

It's 100 percent, right now.
Everything you need is right here.
Everything, the whole Universe, contained in this moment.

Start with one minute.
Then try two.

Being is the way.
There is no other path.

> *Everything you need is right here.*

What if everything you need right now is here? What if everything you need tomorrow will be created for you? What if you could let go and trust and surrender to your reality as soul?

If You're Not Blissed Out, You're Not Paying Attention

The mind will tell you one thing or the other: what you don't have, what you think you need, why this isn't good, why that isn't enough.

In reality, this feast of life is only bliss, nirvana, the shuddering of pure grace.
It is ecstasy, to become aware of this life!
This nectar of the sky, the winds, the air!
This ecstasy of the earth, the plants, the stones!
This grand expanse of earth: all of it and all it contains!

Created by Light, for your immersion and your enjoyment.
Created by Light, so you as Light can be here and feel it.

So you can feel it all, with your bare feet on the ground and your lungs gasping in that sweet air, your arms outstretched to become one with the trees, the birds singing in your ears.

And this is just one moment!

The next moment: the rub of you and all humanity, on a bus, on a subway, all those hearts beating, all that awareness, the continuous pounding of one soul, One Soul, in a space together, everyone feeling and knowing what everyone feels and knows!

Don't pretend you can't feel it.
Don't pretend you don't know.
You're one of One.
You're as one of One as anyone.

Separation is myth. It's myth and myth alone.
Oneness is 24/7 together. This is what Oneness is!
Pure bliss, this ecstasy of One soul, collective soul.

And there is more.

The taste of a papaya, an apple—who could imagine these things?
The feeling of skin on skin, in affection, in healing, in sex?
The entire nervous system attuned to everything, when a sudden rain arrives and washes you clean?

This is the true baptism: the very sky opening up and pouring down upon you, liquid grace.

If you aren't feeling this: why not?

What purpose does it serve you, to stay asleep, to stay constrained, to stay distracted, to stay numbed?

What purpose does it really serve you, to march along the minutes of your life, your entirely ecstatic life, and not allow this ecstasy? Why huddle in the dark corner saying no, no, no, when the feast is here, and you are invited?

The feast is of everything, every single thing, for you to partake of and experience and taste and enjoy. The feast is of everything, every single thing, to send you into feelings of bliss and delight that allow you to cross over into new dimensions, and allow you to live in these new dimensions of consciousness, expansion, love.

And when you feel the no, no, no?
Quiet it as you might a sullen child.

Hook in, latch on, attach, open, cross over, remember.
This place, this bliss, is your reality as often as you like.
You can choose it any time, and you can choose it all times.

But it is up to you, to remember to wake up.
It is up to you, to choose.

This place, this bliss, is your reality as often as you like.

If you're not blissed out, you're not paying attention.

We say, pay attention.

There is not one minute to waste.

Close your eyes. Breathe and relax. When you open them, see if your attention is drawn to something, such as a person, animal, or object. Don't force it. Just let your eyes wander and roam until you feel pulled to something—until you notice what you are noticing. Now let your attention engage with what you are drawn to: really feel it. What is the Universe trying to tell you with this simple act of noticing?

The Burning Bush

It can get really hot where I live in Oregon—heat waves where it's too hot to go out, too hot to even move.

Thus, it didn't make sense one hot August afternoon in the middle of a scorcher, mercury pushing 105, that I was compelled to go outside.

Something was calling me. Something was beckoning. A sort of opening in the field of possibilities, as if anything might happen.

Stepping outside into the suffocating heat, tree crickets clicking and droning, I was drawn to a particular fir tree, towering two hundred feet high. And at my feet, a river of sap pooled from the exposed roots: sticky, bubbly, molten, flowing all over the ground. I stared at it, sweltering in the heat shimmering on my skin, captivated by this river of sap pouring out, when suddenly POW! Everything exploded at the top of the tree.

Spontaneous combustion? Hive in swarm? Burning bush? I was too busy ducking to find out.

When I finally looked up, something like confetti was swirling down from the sky: paper light, pod-winged, tiny flecks floating down in dizzying circles, until they finally landed at my feet.

They were seeds.

Hundreds of seed pods launched into the air by a spontaneous combustion of heat and sap.

Infinite blessings of promise and hope. Manna from the sky.

And, for me, a reminder of how when we are in exactly the right place at exactly the right time, the most unusual things happen in this Universe.

All we have to do is hear the call—and answer it.

When we do this—when we head outside for no reason at all during the dog days of summer—we find ourselves in exactly the right place at the right time, fully in position to witness miracles.

PART FIVE

Surrendering to Everything

24/7

When I first started waking up my sensitivity was a problem.

Lots of folks experience this: empaths who feel too much, intuitives who sense it all, introverts who crave quiet—all of you sensitives and seekers and mystics out there who feel it all, all the time.

Back then, I used to believe I needed to hide away, to be reclusive, to catch a break from this 24/7 interconnection that is the energy of the world.

Until I realized it doesn't work that way.

When you're awake, it's 24/7. A simple trip to the grocery store becomes a profound spiritual experience. There's nowhere to run, nowhere to hide.

It all just is.

I'm picking out a jar of salsa when I spot a friend I haven't seen in years, and I realize that she is beaming light.

The woman who checks out my groceries with the slightly crooked teeth and the gentle smile is the most beautiful soul I've ever seen.

The homeless man outside the store with his bike and his backpacks is engulfed with light.

Even those who show up shrouded in their pain, their anxiety, their issues, their dramas? They're sparking light too.

They're all souls in this world, and once you have seen them, it is impossible not to. And it's not just the souls: it's all objects, energies, things—the salsa jars, the shopping bags, the grocery carts.

All of it singing in chorus, *love, love, love*, as I load my bag into the car and drive home.

I didn't used to want to see things this way. I wanted to hide out and deny it, to protect myself from all this energy, this empathic burden of feeling everything all the time.

Now, I've surrendered.

Every vibration resonates with every other vibration ad infinitum and there is no break. There is no possibility of a break.

It's always happening, this Universe. It's 24/7.

Everything's alive, interconnected, One. Same as it ever was.

It's just that now, we're starting to see it.

LESSON 26

You Are Meant to
Live Embodied

• •

One of the reasons we have bodies is so we can feel.

If you have danced freely, bare feet on the ground, all thought gone, only a swirling spiral of music . . . you know what it is to live embodied.

If you run or walk or do yoga or lift weights—not because you "should" but because it feels good—you know what embodiment is.

If you have sex, fully and freely, without mind, shame, or culture getting in the way, you become embodied.

When you eat, fully and freely, without shame or restriction, you become embodied.

These are human pleasures, meant for you to feel fully, to enjoy!

116

And sometimes in embodiment, there is pain.

If you have birthed a child; if a baby has been created in your body and you have borne this child from your body . . . you know what it is to have the complete experience: pain into joy in your body.

If you injure yourself or have an accident or illness or surgery, pain can be sudden or chronic . . . and the body gnaws on this feeling, and this brings a new understanding of the body.

If your body changes shape or condition: if you get bigger, smaller, stronger, weaker, more youthful, older . . . this brings a new understanding of the body.

The body reminds you, every day, of the great joy it is to have a body.
The body reminds you, every day, of your mortality in this lifetime.

Your soul is not mortal. But the body: the container accompanies you from birth to death with all its changes and shifts and experience—now young and strong, now old and weak, so that you can feel everything, the whole time.

> *The body reminds you, every day, of the great joy it is to have a body.*

When you are in your young body, you can experience. The same is true of the other bodies you will inhabit: the old body, the slim body, the fat body, and so on.

So many ways to feel!

Never one body, not really. For the body changes every day, every month, every year. And as the body changes, so too does the experience.

Most of your suffering is in your head: the mind chatter of how it should be.

Get in your body, as it is right now.
No changes, no improvements, no youth serum.

Get out of your head and get into this body, the body you are in right this minute, and enjoy it completely.

That's what it's there for.

⚘ ⚘ ⚘

How do you feel about your body? Do you compare it to other bodies? Or do love yourself exactly as you are? Do you run your body ragged, or do you care for it with love? How would your life change, if you let yourself cherish your body?

If You Don't Like How You Feel, Feel More

• •

We return to the subject of numbing, distraction, of trying to not be here.

You are here.
You are One.

You can't escape it, ever. Even after this lifetime, there will be another and another. There is no escape from suffering until you learn to transcend, and then to transmute, pain.

To move beyond pain.

Most of us do not consider it is possible to move forward in this way, in this lifetime. Full enlightenment may not be our destiny, this time around.

And yet . . . we can suffer less.
We can feel more joy.

We can become more connected to everything.
We can feel more joy.

To do this, we must step away from distraction, and allow ourselves to feel all that we feel, over and over again.

In this way, there is a great breaking of the human heart, the great cracking open from pain into Light. This expansion from pain into compassion into connection into love. All of it, happening so quickly sometimes, it is one fluid feeling.

From darkness to Light.
From suffering into peace.

To do this, the first step? You must allow yourself to feel.

If something is uncomfortable, allow it.
If something creates anxiety, admit it.
If you feel unsettled, worried, depressed, angry, whatever it is: own it.

Don't be afraid of feeling.
Don't distract or numb or put on a front or try to be brave.
Feel what you feel.
This is your reality, right now.

Don't let your culture tell you differently.
Don't let group thought convince you otherwise.
Don't let your own Misbeliefs mislead you.

The mind is limited; facts are not the whole story.

What you feel determines your perception, creates your reality.

So, feel what you feel.
Go deeper still, and feel what you feel beneath that feeling.
And so on, beneath that.
Until you get to a core or a truth or a knowing.

> *What you feel determines your perception, creates your reality.*

You will know it when you feel it.
Your heart will crack open, just a little bit, as it releases into this truth.

If you don't like what you feel, feel more.
This release into core truth, into core knowing, into your soul truth . . . frees you beyond eternity.

Every human has experienced deep pain and wounding. If there is something you have been avoiding, feeling, or remembering, let yourself feel it now. Simply allow the pain and feeling, letting it move through you until you get to the other side. On the other side is love.

You Can't Get Here from There

Do you want to live from your soul, to live in freedom as who you really are?

We say, you can't get here from there.

You can't get to Now, to being, to consciousness, from the path that society has mapped for you.

That map won't take you here.

When you march purposefully forward on society's map, given to you by family, culture, group thought . . . this path doesn't take you to your true destination. You can strive along this pre-scribed path all you like but it won't take you where you really want to go.

It's all just hurrying up to go nowhere.

Yet when you walk your own path, in your own way, without regard for what society thinks, but only following the nudges of the Universe, leading you ever further on a tantalizing path of self-discovery . . . you arrive as soon as you begin.

You hurry slowly.
You notice everything.
You experience it all.

This is all we're here for. There's nowhere else we need to go.

You relax and breathe and look around you. You have arrived.

What about your goals, your lists, your dreams? Have those if you want. But achievements checked off will never mean as much as the true experience of being here Now, and enjoying what is.

For a while you might find it important: even more items checked off your bucket list. As if achievements, running around the globe doing this and that, will make you feel better, stronger, happier. Yet in reality, the presence of attention you bring to your life is what makes you feel better.

It is not the new that is important.
It is the presence.

You can hold this presence anywhere.
In fact, this is what you are here to learn: the ability to drop into Nowness, wherever you are, whenever, whatever your experience.

Living from soul.
Living in Now.
Aware of everything.
Heart bursting open.

And so we say, drop the map society has given you. Take up your own path, the one you are drawn to wander and explore.

Be in your life, because it is your life.
Do what you do, because you have decided that you must.
Not because society says you must.
Because you demand it of you.

You can't get here with a map that's not your own.
You can only find what you seek—connection, expansion, joy—with your own map.

Your map may lead to achievements, experiences, newness, bucket lists, globetrotting, at first.
But when you get to a certain place of understanding, you'll find the map has changed.

> *Drop the map that society has given you. Take up your own path.*

It takes you only to this moment, fully experienced.
It takes you only to this next moment, fully experienced.
Fully present, as your life's path.
The heart can be opened anywhere on earth.

Do the achievements, the adventures if you like.

They won't matter once you've done them.
Another tick on another box.
While your soul requires only full presence.

Make a list of your dreams and goals, and mark what you've accomplished, what you've let go of, and what you're still working on. Now, take a break and go outside in nature. Notice how you feel in the natural world: relaxed, expanded, at peace. Do you notice the difference between achieving and presence? Can you sense the difference in how you feel?

High Water. Road Closed.

I am a connoisseur of the small, simple pleasures.

Not for me—the rowdy, raucous adventure! It's unlikely that you'll ever read about my bungee jumping exploits, or my climbs up Mount Everest, or how I swam with dolphins, or survived Baja. Small and simple is plenty big enough for me.

So, it was with a genuine thrill that on a winter's bike ride at an eight-hundred-acre wildlife reserve near my home I pushed past the cautionary sign ("High Water, Road Closed") and biked on.

Of course, the Universe is always sending us signs.

But from experience I knew that this sign was not saying "stop." It was calling to me to continue!

The High Water sign goes up like clockwork every fall, when the river along the park starts to rise. And it's true, there are days when the lower paths will be submerged in several feet of water. But other days, you'll come across nothing more than a small puddle, just an inch or two deep—certainly something a person on a bike can handle. And on this blustery day, I was certain that murky puddle was no more than two inches deep—three tops!

Everything was going great as I coasted through nice and easy, until suddenly those two, or maybe three inches, turned out to be twelve, murky, muddy, sloshy, sticky, and my thrill turned to panic and, of course, the bike slid and I plunged my left foot down deep in the drink, and then my right foot followed, and within seconds I was mired to my knees.

Wet.

Muddy.

Grinning.

I wasn't upset. In fact . . . I was exhilarated. Something about that surprising muddy moment woke me up. I took it all in: the pale sky, the cold fields, and my squelching shoes.

"Now, it's getting interesting," I shouted, as I regained my balance and pushed on through more puddles toward the river.

But what I really meant was: "Now, I am awake! Now, I'm here! Now, I'm paying attention!" Now, I'm in Now.

And when I reached the river, I saw the reason I'd snuck past that sign in the first place: a gigantic American bald eagle, so close I could see the white of his head, swooping in the air currents above.

Glorious. Even in muddy shoes.

PART SIX

Becoming Free

Rolling in the Deep

I've been playing a bit of electric bass lately.

We rearranged the downstairs room, and suddenly, the Fender that usually hides in the corner was calling my name. I picked it up and powered up the amp and this big deep sound came out like thunder, and I knew something had begun.

Even though I'm certainly no expert and haven't had much training, I've been around music for a while. I've sung and played percussion and even a bit of keyboard. But it's funny . . . that bass, sitting there patiently in the corner all those years, never entered my consciousness. It's like it was invisible to me: outside my range of possibility.

Until, here we are—and I can't get enough of it.

It's all about the next step on my particular soul path: a longing to roll in the deep.

Vibrationally, the bass is buzzy and big and you feel it in your body. That means it lets you slip under the melody, play alongside the harmony. The bass is the undertone, the wave that builds and crashes under everything, the drone tone that holds the space.

Which means, you don't have to be in the spotlight to play the bass. You don't have to be entertaining, like the melody. You don't have to amp up the energy, like percussion. You don't have to be upbeat and supportive, like so many other accompaniments.

You just hold the power, steady and low, and feel into the heart of the song. You roll in Now.

It's interesting to see what music, what instruments, we are attracted to at different times in our lives as we work out different aspects of our soul growth.

Music is vibrational, energetic, and emotional. When we play, or even when we listen, we are freed and we are healed.

Becoming free. It's all about opening to everything: the person, the situation, the one low note held steady until your whole body thrums along.

You Can Waste an Entire Life in Pain

When you become self-determined you move toward self-actualization. Meaning, you do not accept the role of victim, even if you are a victim.

You notice this as an experience. You understand that the pain and suffering you feel is no different; no bigger, no stronger, no worse, no more profound; than the pain and suffering felt by some being, anyone, at any time.

You accept yourself as one of One and you understand that, even with your particular pain and suffering, you are not alone.

Others are in the abyss right now.
Others are feeling pain right now.
Others are recovering, working through, healing right now.
Others are walking away from abusers, from pain, from darkness right now.

You will experience pain until you learn to transcend it. This understanding may be many lifetimes away for many of you. And at the same time: understanding what you can of pain, of suffering, even now, just a little bit of understanding, will help you move further into peace.

When you experience pain—when you are wronged, or victimized, or betrayed—know that this has happened. Feel it fully. Claim it as yours.

But don't stay stuck there.

Especially when the wound is in childhood—when you are an innocent, a being of pure joy and remembering—and your innocence is stolen from you.

Don't stay stuck there.
Don't let this experience, dark and difficult as it may be, define you.

Consider this experience as one experience among the millions, even billions, you will have in this lifetime.

The pain shows you what pain is. You decide if you're going to carry it with you for your life; if it's going to be the human self you wear, the ego and the personality you put on; if this pain is going to be the way you show up.

Remember, you're one of One. What you feel, everyone feels. What everyone feels, you feel.

Why is it so, that pain and suffering exist? Because not all humans are enlightened.

It is true, you can only manage your own understanding, your own enlightenment. Each soul must walk its own path.

And so, this pain you feel, you as One, is the pain of all souls. Until all are lifted, until all feel no pain; you, and all the others—who are also you—will feel.

What affects the smallest of us, affects all of us.
This is what Oneness means: there is no separation, not from you and God/One/Divine/All.
And not from you and everyone else.

In order to transcend your pain, you must own your victimhood.
Speak out, claim it.
Name it as it is.

And then, in order to transmute your pain into something new, hold compassion.

What affects the smallest of us, affects all of us.

Hold compassion for the victim, who is locked in darkness.
Hold compassion for the perpetrator, who is locked in darkness.
Hold compassion for the brutalized and the brutal, a dance of darkness.

Don't be lofty.
Don't be righteous.

You have been on both sides of the coin in many lifetimes.
Know this clearly.

It is not yours to forgive; this is not your role.
Who is in charge of another soul, for walking on their soul path?

It is only yours to feel compassion for both the Self and the other who are part of the One.

And when you are ready . . . let go of the victim role, of your attachment to pain, of your attachment to darkness and drama and victimhood.

Enough to have these experiences in your lifetime!
You don't need to carry them further, once they are done.

Give yourself this freedom.
Let the past be no longer; not in your mind, not in your heart.
Let the healing of Now move through you: this new miracle, then this next new miracle.
Open to what else life has in store for you.

We understand this is difficult. Let go of victimhood? Let go of abuse? Let go of war and starvation and disease and poverty and grief? In the past, "victim" was the role that was carried from one generation to next to next, all down the lineage.

We say, the time for this, the carrying forth of pain, the passing of pain as karmic burden, is done.

Be free.

Allow others to be free.

Know these experiences, and then move beyond them. And when you have moved beyond them, look back only to lend a hand to those who rise up after you. In this way, you are all lifted together.

As One, you will all experience pain, until none of you experience pain.

This idea that pain is required by you, that you must suffer, over and over and over again? Free yourself from this Misbelief, and your suffering will not exist. For a life wasted in suffering, bitterness, and blame is not what you are here for.

Move beyond pain, into your own enlightenment.

What parts of your life are you wasting in pain? How does this serve you? Does it hold you back? If you were to let go of your pain, what do you think would happen?

You Can Waste an Entire Life in the Past

Memories are not as useful as we believe.

In this society, we document everything: this is my life, in photos, in words.
We document as if to show that we were here, as if we need proof!

We are so busy documenting, we forget to live!

In past generations too, in the lineage, we were told over and over: this is how it was, this is how we were. But in fact, this is only a perception of how it was. When we look closer, we see there are many sides to a memory.

There is no point in over-documenting the past.
There is no point in staying in sentimentality, in memory, in "Auld Lang Syne."

This happened, that happened. Why attach to then, when already the new Now is here?

Your children are beautiful, the time you had with them was beautiful.
Yet even as they grow, you know: they are meant to grow.
Your body as a young body, this body was beautiful.
Yet even as you age, you know: you are meant to age and change.

The relationship you so enjoyed, this relationship was so important.
Yet even at that relationship's end, you know: life is brimming with love.

Life is infinite, everything happens at once, all dimensions and all realities are always Now.
The past is just one realm, a mist of experiences that you have already experienced.

You can't hold on to past experiences any more than you can grasp the future.

You can't hold on to past experiences any more than you can grasp the future.

Again, the moment you recognized as a peak experience: beautiful, glorious, beyond expression. In the middle of that moment, you think: how could there be anything more than this?

And yet, years later, you experience a moment in ordinary time, a morning in which you drank tea in the dim dawn, that was also a beautiful moment.

Or an afternoon, also ordinary and usual, when you stood on the subway with all of humanity and felt it all and knew yourself as part of everything, all at once.

Or an evening in a regular week in a regular month, when you stepped out into the night and were dazzled by the stars above.

All of this profound, gorgeous, memorable, amazing!

Not just the past.
Not just the memories.
Not what you once experienced.
But each moment, right now.

And thus, to hoard memories as if they were gold: to recall the glory days of this and that, even while your present fades and is lost before you . . . this is not the way to live.

Don't waste your life wishing for what was.
Don't waste your life thinking the best is over.
Don't waste your life in regret for actions taken or untaken.

Dry your sentimental tears.
Do not look back a moment longer.

This is Now, a new moment!
All possibility is yours, when you choose to create it.
This moment holds all you need.

Do you have certain memories that you return to again and again? Close your eyes, and take a quick run through of the memories you often remember. You might notice a memory from your childhood, from your adulthood, from the age you are currently. Now, let your mind wander to a few memories you don't often remember—let yourself be surprised by what shows up! Even if these are good memories, do you see that the past can only show the person you used to be—not the person you are now, or the person you are becoming?

Failure Is Growing

You have arrived on this earth, soul in human container, with this many or that many years ahead of you for one reason.

To learn to live.

Not in a small way: a puny life of shame and fear and pain.
Not in a middling way: a careful life without risk, without reward.
Not in a reckless way: burning all bridges the moment you cross them.

But with eyes open, heart open.

Willing to connect, engage, learn, expand, grow.
Willing to make mistakes, mess up, stumble, lose.
Willing to fail, fail again, fail even further.

All failure is growing.

When we step forward, it is new; how could we know what to do, how could we know how it works, until we've done it a time or two?

And thus, all life is practice, all life is learning.
One lesson after another.
The progressive curriculum of pain, compassion, connection, love.
One lesson after another, learning as we go.

Why be hard on yourself, when you fail?
Why have the enormous ego response to failure?
Why expect yourself to be better, bigger, stronger than anyone else?

We're each incredibly flawed.
We're each astoundingly perfect.
We each hover around darkness.
We each burn with radiant Light.

We are "all that": the all of it, all the time.

Why expect to be good?
Why expect to be Light without shadow?
Why expect to learn before you do the lesson?

In learning to live, you will fail many times.
There may be no time you will not be failing!
Humble yourself to this expectation.
Appreciate this grace, that you can begin again, and again, and again.

There is no time you cannot open further.
There is no time you cannot learn more.
There is no time you cannot experience Light.

This gift of learning without end: it
is your road to enlightenment.
Stay on the path.
You'll never not fail.

> *This gift of learning without end: it is your road to enlightenment.*

Laugh, enjoy, humble yourself.
Become perfectly imperfect!
This is the path: not a straight
line, but a crooked one with many
opportunities to look at the view,
to see how far you've come, to continue in the wrong direction, and to come back home, again and again, to your true path.

Don't worry about failing.
It's part of the journey.

What is your experience with failure? Have you failed many times, as most of us have? Or have you played it safe, and not let yourself fail? What has failure taught you so far? What lessons are you especially glad you learned? What would you like to risk next? What calls you?

The Mystery Beckons

Society tells you that you need a map. A map of your life, that you're meant to follow without stopping, from birth to death, beginning to end.

We say, this is society's map.
We say: in this life of living from soul, you're going to have to throw this map away.

You're going to have to walk blind.
You're going to have to walk without knowing where you're going.
You're going to have to let go of all expectation of achievement, measurement of success, all the ways you mark progress.

The great leap is not into the known.
The great leap is into the mystery.

The mystery, and you the mystic!

> *The great leap
> is not into the
> known.
> The great leap is
> into the mystery.*

The mystery, and you the soul explorer!

When you choose to walk toward illumination, it's so bright it can be blinding. All around you, the dimly lit path of the ordinary way, the regular way, the way society wants you to walk.

But get up here in the Light! How can you even see one step ahead of you? The Light so bright it blinds all.

The mystery of what's next is a gift to you from the Universe.

How dull, to have it mapped out!
How dull, to follow someone else's, society's map!

How incredible! What passion, what gift, what deep joy to set out on the path of the unknown, with the only direction and directive that you will be true to your soul Self; that you will live from soul, and you will let soul lead.

This commitment to living from soul will take you on an unexpected journey, whether you travel the world or you stay at home. Whether you meet many people, or only a few. Whether you achieve worldly success, or live a simple life. Yet in all cases, this walking on the path in your own way, throwing away the map and letting the Light lead . . . this is walking in the mystery, and it is the sweetest, most profound way to live a life!

Take your map out. Look at where they told you that you needed to go.

Now, throw the map away and start walking.

Your soul knows the way.

Think back to a time when you had no idea where you were going but you still found your way. What it did feel like, to walk fully in the mystery? To let go of all maps and rules, and let the Universe be your guide? Are you ready to walk in this way again? Which way do you feel inspired to go?

Living from Your Soul

The human self is here to serve the soul.

So often in worldly life, this aspect is confused.
Instead, we let the body lead, the personality lead, the ego lead.
These are not the right leaders!

Only the soul can guide.
Only the soul shines light.

The human self . . . this is merely the vessel, the vehicle by which the soul experiences everything.

The human container is important, for this is how we see, hear, and feel in our embodied state.
It is the greatest gift to be in body, for without our human container we are just Spirit: untethered, amorphous, etheric.

We are uncontained.

We are infinite Light.
We can't feel it all.

And yet because our container is so important, because it gives us the gift of feeling everything, we think it is in charge. But consider, the container you inhabit as a baby changes into the container you inhabit as a teen.

The emotions, personality, and ego change.
The emotions become less virulent.
The personality less insistent.
The ego less demanding.

And the body changes also: the wild ups and downs, the love and the hate of life, all of this mellows into an acceptance, a knowing, a realizing of the body for what it is, and what it is not.

Different ages.
Different stages.
Different expressions of personality, ego.
Different containers of body.

And through this all: the soul leads. The soul . . . this aspect of Oneness that is you, that you are part of, this true Self that is above all containers, that will exist in millions of containers in millions of lifetimes, that will experience millions of personalities and egos in millions of experiences . . . the soul leads.

The soul leads you on the journey of remembering your true Self. All else falls by the wayside, as you journey deeper and deeper, higher and higher, into this understanding.

You are here to learn how to live as soul in human container, in the highest, most experiential, most present way you can.

Let all else drop away.
Live from your soul.

You have millions of years to learn these lessons.
We say, enjoy it all.

Enjoy your body, in whatever shape it is.
Enjoy your personality, with all its flaws.
Enjoy the very struggles themselves, as they open you.

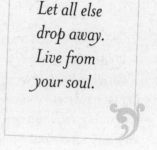

Let all else drop away. Live from your soul.

Look! The Light is dawning.
Feel! Your heart is cracking open.
Be in awe of every moment.
In this life, for whatever moments you have left, let your soul lead.

What would happen if you let go of all the fear and pain and Misbelief, and began to live in the fullest, most authentic, present, and loving way you could? Is anything stopping you from living like this now?

We Leave with Nothing

There's something very strange going on with my purse.

It's becoming empty over time.

For decades, I've worn a cross-body bag. When you are raising four kids and you have to fasten a baby into a car seat while restraining a squirming toddler while stopping another kid from kicking a soccer ball while saying "no" to the teen who wants to drive . . . well, you need to have your hands free.

Back in those years, my purse was packed: cheese sticks, binkies, spare diaper, random doll, cell phone about five times the size of my current one, ring of keys as hefty as those carried by Tower of London guards. Lipstick maybe, and a hairbrush. And a pen and, of course, my journal.

Nowadays, most of that life is done.

I'm down to a wallet. My phone. Three keys.

It's funny how when we're younger we are so excited to have these things to carry. These signs of adulthood, and of our life suddenly forming: our ID, our keys, our money, our phone, our debit card.

Later still, we're so grown up that we get to carry stuff for every single role we're playing: briefcase, laptop, gym bag, protein bar.

And then one day . . . we're down to practically nothing.

We arrive with nothing.

We leave with nothing.

The contents of my purse show me that I am moving through the cycles of my life, as you are with yours.

Book II

The Universe Speaks

PART SEVEN

Direct Connection

One Drop More

Many summers ago when my children were young, we'd pull out the plastic paddling pool, drag it out onto the lawn, and fill it with water from the hose. When the pool was full, but before they jumped in and started to splash around, we'd add color.

A few drops of blue or yellow or green or red from the McCormick's food coloring kit kept with the baking supplies. One color only, chosen by kids' consensus, one drop at a time.

One drop!

One drop more!

It was the highlight of the paddling pool!

It was interesting how many drops it took: one drop of yellow didn't make a difference, two drops didn't change anything, three or four did nothing . . . all the way up to twenty-three drops, before we witnessed a transformation. Finally, on the twenty-fourth drop, the water would take on the faintest tinge of yellow. It was that twenty-fourth drop that did it . . . that was the tipping point, when change happened.

The kids would cheer in excitement, and we'd add more drops as the water got brighter and more saturated with color, and then everyone would jump in and cool off and slosh around and pour water on each other's heads.

Ahh . . . summer.

It's interesting how one little drop can make so much of a difference. It's all ordinary water . . . until one drop more, and it's not.

Our connection with the Universe is like this too.

We become more Divine every time we are in communion with the energetic expression of the Universe/God/One/All, in all the forms this can take.

Just like the yellow food coloring, one more drop can make all the difference: one more meditation session, one more prayer, one more walk in nature, one more moment of full presence. One little drop can raise us from mostly human to mostly soul, in any given situation.

One drop more to shift the balance from mundane to Divine. One drop more of this sweet nectar, as easy to obtain as closing your eyes, taking a deep breath, and asking to receive.

The kids are grown, the paddling pool's long been given away.

But it's still there in memory: how we saw with our own eyes the exact moment the water changed: clear to sunny yellow; a transformation caused by one drop more, long ago on a summer day.

The Two-Fold Path

You desire to become intuitive, because you know it is possible.

In your heart, you understand clearly that intuition is something attainable, not a gift only for a chosen few. You know it's your birthright. It's part of who you are! It's how you are created, as soul-in-human body!

The practice of spiritual intuition teaches you how to unlock your intuition, how to open your "windows" so the Universe may reach you easily, simply, every day, at all times.

The purpose of this practice is to give you direct connection with all the Divine guides and mentors who work endlessly to guide you to your highest possibility. And so that you may grow into the consciousness that brings direct knowing: the knowing of all, just because you are.

This is where an interesting understanding comes to you: intuition is a spiritual path.

You can travel on the road of intuitive learning, taking courses and teachings and learning different skills. And if you travel this road deeply and with humility, you will end up spiritually awake.

The spiritual path leads to intuition.

It is just what happens when you are in direct connection for any length of time, over time.

Conversely, the spiritual path leads to intuition. If you travel on the path of spiritual growth long enough, doing whatever practices of meditation, prayer, renunciation, tradition . . . no matter which religion or practice you do . . . you will end up opening your intuitive self.

Consciousness is the result of intuition.
Intuition is the result of consciousness.

It is a two-fold path, and you may begin to walk it from either direction: the intuitive side of direct connection, or the consciousness side of direct knowing.

This is of course the path of the spiritual psychic, in which you walk both sides of the path, in which you travel the two-fold path at both times. You understand that your intuition arrives from your spiritual practice, and so you steep yourself deeply in mystic practice. You understand that your consciousness arrives from intuitive practice, and so you also, and at the same time, steep yourself deeply in direct connection with the guides, angelic realms, and others who guide you and bring you intuitive information.

All of this is done in the highest vibration.
All of this is done with love.
All of this is done as your journey of soul growth, in your quest to be free.

Recall a recent time that your intuition suddenly opened, a time when you just "knew"? What if this deep knowing was available to you anytime, anywhere—whenever you are connected to the Divine?

No Middleman Required

There has been a myth in society, of the chosen few.

This idea some of you are better than others, or more capable than others when it comes to the intuitive arts.

This is not so.

Each of you is born with the inalienable birthright of your own soul. As such, your soul is not just "part of you." Your soul is you.

Your soul inhabits your body, your personality, your circumstance, in the same way you might get into a car and drive it.

In some lifetimes, you choose a luxury vehicle. In others, a junker ready for the junk yard. In others, a car that drives with utmost reliability and lack of problem.

You drive all these different cars in different lifetimes; some of you will choose to drive several different cars in this lifetime alone.

By cars, we do not just mean the physical structure, the container that is the human body.

By cars, we mean the all of it, the package as it were: the body, the personality, the ego with its demands, the time, the place, the culture, the environment.

All the ways you show up in the world.

The point is that you, as soul, are the driver. You, your soul, creates your entire experience in this and all lifetimes, just as you, the driver, determine where your car goes.

This idea that you need a middleman to help you understand your soul's path? It is Misbelief, it is incorrect, it is ridiculousness, born of centuries of the need for religious, cultural, and political bodies to control individuals. It is born of centuries of group thought. It is born of centuries of souls giving away their inalienable birthright and choosing to believe someone else has the key, the secret, the map, the path.

You have the key.

No one else.

This is your journey—no middleman required. No priest, no guru, no spiritual teacher. No celebrity, no expert, no leader.

The Divine offers much higher holies, much more radiant light.

Light your path with this bright burning!

Discern carefully!

Anyone who seeks to control or coerce is not a right teacher. Anyone who uses fear, shame, or guilt is not a right teacher!

Work only with those who help you see your own Light. Seek only those who help you to have direct connection with the highest Divine.

You may be supported, and you may support along the way. But in the end, it is your own path to walk. The soul's quest is an individual journey, and it is not clearly marked. It is walking in the mystery, from birth unto death, as the cycle repeats again.

The mystery becomes more and more clear, as you journey on your soul path. Your destination is to experience yourself as God/One/All.

This may take many years.
Or it might happen today.

The Universe will light your path, when you stop giving your power away to others and to group thought.

This is your journey—no middleman required.

You will be shown clearly, when you trust your own soul.

How does it change your thinking to understand that no middle-man is required between you and the Universe? Is this scary—or is it freeing? How does it change your belief system—what you were taught to believe, what your family believes, what others around you believe? What happens when you begin to accept that you already have the key, the secret, the map, and the path?

Direct Connection Is Yours

As a soul, you are God.

The smallest particulate of you is God. The entire auric field of you is God.

By God, we do not mean God as you may know "Him" from your childhood or your culture. We mean the ineffable One/All/Divine/Source/Universe that is part and parcel of all souls.

You as soul are God.
You as collective soul are God.
Collective soul as Universe is God.

This is true for the smallest energy particulate; this is true for the infinite Universe.

You cannot separate yourself from this reality.
You cannot take the God part out of yourself.

You cannot become not One.

Now, you can turn away from your true essence, and many of you do. You turn away from pain, fear, distraction, addiction, group thought. . . . There are so many distractions in the human life that may cause you to turn away.

This is why we bring your attention again and again to your true essence, your true identity, your true Light.

You have heard the tales of Jesus, sitting down with thieves and prostitutes? And loving them, regardless of their sins, the way they went against their culture?

Jesus did this because he knew: all are holy, all are Divine, all are made of God.

This is where many of you are now: human containers of addictions, distractions, shame, fear, pain, anger. . . . And yet, even with all this in your outer being, your inner being remains the same: pure light, pure One, pure God.

> *You cannot take the God part out of yourself. You cannot become not One.*

Is it better to be "good"? Is it more holy? We say, not always. Goodness implies cultural Misbelief. What is "good" in one culture may be "bad" in another.

What is most important is to wake up to your true nature. When you awaken to your true essence, all the old habits and Misbeliefs drop away!

The Light leads all.

The key to waking up is to open to us, meaning us in particular: the many guides and angelic beings who are direct translators for you of the ineffable grace of God/One/All/Universe.

We are here to assist you. We are here to translate the exquisite language of the Universe for you. We are here to bring pure Light as you raise your vibration to the radiance you are able to bear as a human, what can be managed by your Self at this time.

As you attach to Light, you become able to attach to more Light.

We ask that you make direct connection with us, your guides and angels. This is the most direct way you can learn to speak the language of the Universe, to begin to shift your vibration, and to begin to lean toward the Light in all aspects of your soul's journey.

Close your eyes. Breathe and relax. Now, ask your guides and angels, direct translators of the Universe, the question that is in your heart. Then stay open for the answer: a message or a feeling or a knowing. It might arrive instantly or be revealed over time. Either way, the answer is coming.

How the Universe Communicates

We bring you back to the path of the spiritual psychic.

This is the path of paying exquisite attention to how the Universe communicates to you as soul in human container. It is, in essence, the path of learning how to speak the language of the Universe.

We must say: this is the language available to all humans living in Light.

We of the other realms understand many different levels of Universal language. But this way that the Universe communicates to you—as soul in human body right now, in your culture, in your time—this understanding is available to you.

Just like any language or skill, you must study it.

Just as with any course of study, you must eliminate distractions and apply the full force of your focus to your understanding.

Just as with the learning of anything, you must have patience, because understanding does not happen at once.

You learn over time.
Your understanding increases.
With study, you begin to understand.
With practice, you become adept.

So it is with spiritual intuition. Sometimes, it is true, there are great jolting openings all at once; you see these in what you call near-death experiences, which are really only moments in which you see your true essence for the first time.

You see this also after great shocks to the system or the pattern that the organism is living: a great loss, illness, divorce, and so forth. This shock disrupts the pattern, interrupts all the Misbeliefs and distractions, so the organism shocks into soul Self; and of course whenever we live from soul, whenever we see from soul perspective, all becomes crystalline.

We see our true essence, as a result of this shock.

However . . . there are gentler ways. These are preferable, as they cause the human organism less stress and allow an easier experience in learning and integration.

When you begin to allow your human self to pay exquisite attention to Now, to be in the present moment fully, all things change.

In this mindfulness of the moment, is a kind of rapture. By this, we mean that everything that was once not noticed, that was pushed away by distractions of all kind, suddenly comes to the forefront.

With the absence of distraction of all kinds, the soul can peek out from the human container and feel everything, all at once.

For example, if you are at home doing chores with the TV or radio on and a house full of people, with your mind full of memories and looping thoughts of how much you have left to do and how little time you have to do it, thus attaching to both past and future . . . the Universe will have a very hard time reaching you in this moment.

And yet, if you put down your chore, or if you do one chore in a quiet, mindful way; if you turn off the TV and the radio; if you create a little space from others; if you deliberately stop the rushing of your mind, then you enter into a dimension of quiet stillness.

Begin to allow your human self to pay exquisite attention to Now.

You are hovering very close to Now.

And if you slow down further and begin to breathe more fully, and if you slow down even more fully and either close your eyes or soften your gaze to take it all in all at once . . . and if you slow down even further and simply suspend all mind chatter and Misbeliefs and judgment and group thought . . . then you begin to notice things you could not see, hear, or feel before:

You begin to notice the beauty of the clock ticking on the wall.

You begin to feel the air on your skin, a delicious comforting breeze.

You begin to feel your own body, the cells in perfect communion.

You begin to see an image, in your mind's eye, and this is a knowing for you.

You begin to sense a memory long forgotten, and this informs you.

You begin to notice an object, and this is an answer to you.

You begin to hear a message, in your mind's ear, and this is an answer to you.

You being to have direct knowing, in which you just know everything.

In this moment, in which you do not worry about result, or answer . . . you have in essence put yourself in the swirl of Universal information.

Every time you allow yourself to go into this great swirling moment of stillness, of Nowness, you become exquisitely able to hear the language of the Universe.

Every time you enter into this realm of Now, which contains all past, all present, all future at all layers and levels, you become more able to hear and understand the constant and continued whisperings of the Universe.

Recall the last time you sat quietly, not doing or thinking, just being. Do you feel how this deep stillness transports you to an expanded reality? What memories, visions, answers, knowings arrive when you are in this space?

Why Vibration Matters

Vibration is another way of speaking about openness, transparency, radiance.

Of opening to your own innate Light.

When we speak of raising vibration, we speak of your willingness to shed Misbeliefs, distraction, and group thought, so that you experience the higher energies of your Divine essence.

Your culture—and we say this for you who find this work at any time in history—your culture makes it very simple for you to stay distracted.

This is the purpose of the culture: to bind you to the group, to create sheep out of souls!

Darkness: the absence of light. All distraction, all Misbelief, all group thought . . . all of this shadows your own innate Light.

When you raise your vibration, you let go of darkness and all that is dark in your life.

Sometimes this is confusing, because your culture celebrates much of its darkness. For example, TV is often dark, movies are often dark, sports are often dark, politics are often dark, celebrity idolatry is often dark . . . and yet the darkness is often revered!

It is part of the human nature, to want to be separate from God. It is the willful, egoic part of you that is human, that turns toward darkness, that praises darkness!

Remember: your soul must walk its own path. Yet once you have a glimpse of consciousness, you see these are false idols, dark distractions, Misbeliefs, group thought.

Remember: your soul must walk its own path.

This means letting go of all the distractions, Misbeliefs, and group thought that you have been taught by your culture, and walking in a higher elevation.

We are not saying to disassociate from your culture! We say, when you come into your true soul Self, you won't be interested in what your culture is doing. Distractions, Misbeliefs, and group thought that you have been taught by your culture will fall away as you walk in a higher elevation.

You will see behind the curtain: you will recognize the machinations as false, and unimportant.

You will see that there is another way to live, one that has nothing to do with what you have been taught to believe.

You will see that you can live in equanimity and compassion, in joy and peace and tranquility.

> *There is another way to live, one that has nothing to do with what you have been taught to believe.*

You will see that you can live free, in this lifetime.

You can raise vibration, turn away from what is dark. If you aren't sure what is dark, see what makes you feel fear, pain, anger, shame, anxiety, or "not enough."

Turn away from all that.

If you aren't sure what is Light, move toward what makes you feel good, whole, safe, and loved. Turn toward that, without hesitation or excuses.

Immerse yourself in that Light.

In what ways does your ego try to keep you separate from God? What if you let your soul lead instead? Can you imagine how your life would change if you did?

Opening Your Windows

We ask that you open your windows!

By this, we mean that you ask to receive Universal information via direct connection, and that you begin the practice of direct connection.

The first step, the asking, requires that you acknowledge your willingness to take this new step on your path of soul growth.

You open to the idea of guides, angels, the Universe all communicating directly, one-on-one with you.

Your willingness: your surrender, your throwing yourself off the cliff into the mystery that is your life . . . this is the asking.

The asking arrives of the heart, for the heart is where the soul resides.

The asking arrives of the heart, the heart's longing for true connection to the Divine.

For so long, so many of you have been crying in the wilderness, seeking this solution and that solution, this distraction and that distraction, when the answer is this: surrender.

> *The heart is where the soul resides.*

Become humble.
Place your ego in the corner and let go of all greed and distraction. Ask for what is true Light. And in asking, you will receive.

The next way we say to you is to open your windows, to begin the practice of direct connection. Without you slowing down for a time each day, or for many times each day, we find it harder to reach you. For those of you who have stubbornly shut your ears, you may find yourself in direct connection only when there are great shocks or disruption!

It does not have to be this way.

Instead, you begin a practice. You sit quietly each day, eyes closed, gently breathing in and out. . . . In this way, we can begin to reach you, and we can raise your vibration and give you the ability to increase your vibration and increase your concentration so that you go further.

In this way, we can begin to communicate with you in ways that you understand, and you open to the endless stream of Universal knowledge that is arriving to you even now.

This sitting practice is only one way. But it is the easiest and most attainable for most of you.

You notice we do not call it meditation?
You notice we do not call it prayer?
You notice we do not call it mindfulness or bhakti or beingness?

All of these are practices, and certainly they are useful. But these words are loaded or triggered with feelings about how things must be done or not done.

We ask you to detach from the idea of "not doing it right."

We ask that you open your windows and you make yourself available to your Divine helpers, and to all of the Universe, and to do this in the simplest way available.

This simplest way to enter in is by stillness. Again, you do not need to sit for long. At the beginning, ten minutes may be all you can manage, before the looping thoughts and crushing world invade your awareness once again.

In asking, the process is begun.
Upon entering in, the veils are lifted.

To read or listen to words and not practice takes you nowhere. It may even be worse than nowhere, as you have the sense of having accomplished something without having the true experience.

When you enter in, the first or the millionth time, your heart cracks open to the Divine.

This entering in, this heart's cracking open, is where you begin again the first time, and where you begin every time henceforth.

Close your eyes and be still. Ask that your windows be opened; that all veils be lifted. Say it in prayer, or say it out loud. Understand that with this asking, you place yourself in direct connection with the Universe. Let your heart crack open, and rest in this space.

The False Path

* *

Many people who desire to become psychic want nothing to do with the Divine.

They want to learn psychic skills to use as tools of ego, for their own advantage, from a place where they can astonish and manipulate others. They want to see the future, to know what will happen next, to understand where the energy is moving in all things; they want to know not out of humility or true desire, but because they think this knowledge will protect them, and keep them from fear and pain.

To attain the siddhis, these kinds of skills, is not important.

The siddhis are about focus, not Light.

Worse still, those who seek to master these siddhis often seek to acquire these tools for their own gain.

Many of the spiritual teachers and leaders in any culture are such as these: they have gained the pinpointed concentration that allows them to master the siddhis, but their hearts have not opened, are not open.

Recall again: the heart is where the soul resides. The soul is Light. The heart cracks open into Light.

Pinpointed focus, and the tricks and techniques of the wizard, the seer, the sorcerer, the magi; these are interesting, but no more than that.

They do not measure enlightenment of a being.

In this way, we ask that you choose to open to the energy of the Divine with the purest heart, the humblest of intention, the longing to move only in the nectar of love.

The siddhis may arrive to you over time and with practice, if you choose to move in that direction.

But without the heart's true longing for grace, they will become the biggest stumbling block for you.

Be cautious on your path. Watch for the false road.

There will be darkness on all sides, at times. There will be temptations as your abilities and as your understanding increases. Darkness has its own silky call, and can be very alluring.

Follow the path of Light. It is your infinite destiny.

What kinds of ego temptations have you faced in your life? What false roads have you walked, until you gained the clarity that they were false? Are there any false roads you are walking on right now? If there are, look at them deeply today, and see if they are what your soul wants.

Follow the path of Light. It is your infinite destiny.

My Little Basil Plant

This summer, which has been mild and mellow here in Oregon, I have enjoyed watering our garden very much.

Each plant has become familiar to me, and I love the practice of giving them a long, thirsty drink; I love the way they go from slightly dehydrated to flush with water.

The familiarity is interesting: there's the rose, there's the zebra grass, there's the black bamboo, there's the green bamboo, there's the clematis, there's the hollyhock, there's the sunflower.

Everything's pretty haphazard; it's a casual garden, and nothing is particularly fancy. But as I've come to know these stalwart and sturdy plants over the years, I've become fond of them.

I've learned to sense their energy, and I have a sense of great friendliness when I am out in the garden: that everyone is chiming in with friendly hellos and good vibes.

To be clear, I do not physically hear the plants. I sense them. I feel them. And I can feel they are friendly, and I can feel the difference of one from another. The sunflowers are different from the roses. The hollyhocks are different from the grasses. And so on.

You feel this too: you know it.

I was especially feeling the love with my little basil plant, so pretty and fragrant, doing such a great job in this mild and mellow summer—this soft, glossy, beautiful plant—and I felt joyous every time I watered it.

Then, the other night at dinner as I popped a bite of garden-fresh pesto into my mouth, I realized with the alarm of a mother who's accidently bitten her baby that I was eating my little buddy. Disclaimer: I'm not vegan, I'm not always vegetarian. Yet this one spoonful of pesto did me in. I ate it, and even as it went into my mouth, I felt everything about that little basil plant: its sweetness and its love, and I put the spoon down in wonder and in shock. It took me a while to understand what was happening.

When we start to wake up, as so many are right now, these unexpected leaps forward in understanding become common; one day it's fine to eat meat, the next it's not. One day dairy is okay, the next it feels sickening. One day it's no big deal to eat a vegetable, the next you're having a full-on spiritual response to the plant, its energy and its essence, even as you're eating it and it's becoming part of your body.

We are all interconnected. There is no way out of this.

There is only the greater understanding of Oneness, becoming clearer every day.

PART EIGHT

Divine Guidance

The White Feather

The Universe is always leaving us clues and signs.

One woman I know discovers crystals near the base of trees: not just now and then, but all the time. Another woman sees feathers everywhere, as if angels are in molting season. Others find the answer they seek in words: they open a random book to a random page, only to find the sentence that correlates to their question. And surely we've all seen signs, literal signs, on the highway of life: Stop! Go! Proceed with caution! Yield!

I often ask the Universe for guidance when I'm walking. In the forest, for example, where I can let myself float in the energy of trees. When I'm in nature I expect natural signs: a deer sighting, an eagle in flight, a cobweb dazzling with dew.

But sometimes, the Universe likes to have fun with us.

On a recent hike with my husband at Silver Falls Park, ninety-two hundred acres of Oregon forest, I asked the Universe what the heck I was supposed to be doing with my life.

It had been a long summer, fraught with uncertainty. Each morning I'd wake up, arrange myself at my desk, and chop-wood-carry-water. I wrote for hours . . . words poured through me and I moved myself aside the best I could. But what's this all for? I'd ask myself. It wasn't clear.

I'd meditate and get "Keep writing."

I'd pray and get "Keep writing."

But it still wasn't clear why.

So, on this late summer hike, I asked the Divine for clear guidance.

"Bring me a sign, and I want it crystal clear—something I can easily understand!" I requested as I started up the trail.

As these things go, I was easily distracted. There was so much to look at! The crashing waterfall that drops 170 feet, the towering ancient firs, the great greenness of everything. I was knee-deep in chlorophyll grace.

We finally stopped at a picnic table beside the stream, and here was the most picturesque setting: the burbling water, the falls below, the trees whispering, everything natural as could be. And as these things happen, there was my sign: a large white feather, right beneath the picnic table. Not an ordinary feather, as if from a robin or blue jay or osprey or eagle from the area. But a foot-long feather, bleached white, sharpened at the end.

"My sign!" I said to my husband. "It must mean . . . hmm . . . I guess it . . . it means . . . uh . . . everything's going to be okay?"

My husband stared at the giant white feather that had dropped from no natural bird anywhere and he started laughing.

"That's no feather," he said. "It's a quill."

The Universe has a sense of humor. The Universe likes to be crystal clear with its signs. A quill, the symbol of writers everywhere, dropped not from a bird but conjured from thin air, in perfect answer to my question.

Guidance Arrives in Visions

There has been a great deal of misunderstanding in your culture of how we communicate with you.

By we, we mean all your guides, the angelic realm, the departed realm, nature, animals, the other dimensions, the energies of higher vibration.

You have the ability, as a soul-based being, to enter into many of these Universe's layers and levels.

It is only your perception that keeps you from these other realities.

Free your mind from Misbeliefs of culture, family, corporation, even your own fear, and it is easy to enter into these other multidimensional Universes. This is what is meant by multidimensional Universe, but we choose to say it more simply: layers and levels.

We always choose to speak more simply, to your child Self, to your heart nature, so you understand more fully. Understand that our language is not yours: the Universe speaks in ways that are beyond your ability, as human, to understand.

Thus, we create a bridge that allows translation.

We, the guides, are your bridge, translating the infinite energy, so that your human aspect can receive it, understand it, and use it. Without this bridge, the energy is too great for your form. It is ultimate radiance, and too strong for your physical being.

With this bridge, and with the help of us balancing and moderating the energy, you can experience so many things!

In this way, we must create a spot of meeting, where our vibration lowers to meet yours, and your vibration raises to meet ours. This meeting point, this point of entering in, is where direct connection happens.

As we have said before, so many of you go well beyond the meeting point, into higher states of radiance and bliss. These are beautiful and healing vibrational points for you, but we say, these spots are too far above the human vibration for you to understand.

It is only immersion, without understanding. This vibrational state is good, valid, and useful. But if you seek understanding, it is not where you need to go.

To reach us most clearly, to enter the space where it is easiest for us to communicate with you in the ways that you understand—language, symbol, vision, sound, emotion—you need to enter at a vibration that is not so distant from your natural state.

We ask that you enter in with eyes closed. We ask that you enter in on the breath. You will feel slightly relaxed, nothing more. You will feel still, and you will feel your heart open.

This is all that is needed for direct connection.

When you are in this space, you will then be able to receive from us in ways that you understand. One of the first ways you will receive from us is in visions.

By this, we mean that you will see things in your physical container, your mind's eye. Less often, you may see visions outside in the layers and levels of the Universe: you may see the veil lift in the physical world. But in most cases, and for most uses, all is shown to you in your mind's eye.

Try this now: close your eyes, breathe, relax, and then allow a vision to come into your mind's eye.

You will be surprised how visions show up; you may feel like you are thinking of something, or a thought will show up in a vision form.

Seeing visions may remind you of how you feel when you are thinking about something, or imagining it, or when you read and you picture something in your mind.

Sometimes the vision is of past, such as a past life.
Sometimes the vision is of past, such as a memory.
Sometimes the vision is of present.
Sometimes the vision is of future in this lifetime.
Sometimes the vision is of future in a future lifetime.
Sometimes the vision is of alternate Universes.

Do you see how visions show up as a function of time? This is one thing to understand, when you look at visions: when in the time continuum they are located.

Do you see how visions show up as a function of expanded time? This is one thing to understand when you look at visions: if they are a part of this present Universe you inhabit as your human reality, or if they are a part of an alternate or parallel Universe that you have entered.

You understand symbols, metaphors, archetypes, and so forth; these are a part of your culture, and part of your way of understanding. Thus, visions are often symbolic: they are shortcuts for us to communicate a vast array of information.

We also show you visions as movies in your mind: these contain movement, progression, and action, allowing you to see the direction a certain relationship or container of energy is taking.

We show you the vision in action, moving toward a destination.

Everything is in relationship, always.
Everything is a container of energy.
Everything is all at once.

> *Everything is in relationship, always. Everything is a container of energy.*

Everything is Now.

When you see a vision in your mind's eye, you see an aspect of the Universe being communicated to you as guidance, to help move you to your highest possibility of soul growth.

What you learn from your vision is related to your consciousness; the more you let go of egoic concerns and distractions, the more clearly you can receive and interpret visions, and the more easily you can follow them without fear or anxiety.

When you receive visions, and this is something you can practice daily, or during your day . . . these are guidance arriving to you, to help Light your way.

Visions show up, messages from Light, to light the way on your soul path.

Consider a question that you'd like to ask the Universe. Close your eyes, breathe, and relax. In a moment, a vision will arrive in your mind: perhaps as a memory, perhaps as a symbol, perhaps as something else. How does this vision relate to your question?

Guidance Arrives in Messages

Some of you hear us in your mind.

You are attuned to language, you are attuned to words, you are attuned to speech, you are attuned to sound.

So this is how we reach you.

Remember: the Universe speaks to you in the language that you best and most easily understand.

Thus, visions will be the primary mode of direct connection for some. Others will receive guidance in messages.

Remember: you receive from your soul.

Thus, the human experience of seeing a vision in the room, or the human experience of hearing a message audibly, as you would in your everyday world . . . this is not how the soul communicates: not with the eye, not via the ear.

The soul receives information in the higher frequencies of Universal vibration, and this shows up to you in your mind's eye, your mind's ear, and your heart.

> *The Universe speaks to you in the language that you best and most easily understand.*

This means, you receive visions from the Universe in your mind's eye.
You receive messages from the Universe in your mind's ear.
You receive knowing from the Universe in your heart.

Recall: the heart is where the soul resides.

When you receive in messages, they may show up in a few ways.

The language that you hear as a human is not usually translatable in receiving. When you hear messages from guides, this is usually a form of telepathy in the mind's ear.

This is the same way you will hear messages from the Departed.

It is not an audible sound in the room, for the most part; although for a tiny portion of you, you will hear audibly. Yet to hear audibly is not better, more advanced, and is not a goal.

To hear in your mind's ear, and to have the ability to separate your own egoic thought from the message itself: this is the task for you!

To be able to hear clearly, the higher understanding of the Universe!

To be able to hear clearly, the sweet whisper of your soul!

It takes some practice to dull your mind chatter, to vanquish your own looping thoughts, the egoic desire, the grasping, the fear, and so forth. This is where stillness without distraction, creating a place of human sensory deprivation so that the thoughts can finally stampede, career, and, eventually, exhaust themselves and become still, allowing the true message to arrive.

Once you have stilled your mind, opened up into no expectation, no desire for outcome, no fear of what you might find there . . . this is where the Universe can reach you.

Once you have freed yourself, even momentarily, from the distraction of the outer world and all its drama and chaos . . . this is the place where the Universe can reach you.

You may find yourself receiving messages when you enter into stillness. Often, messages come unexpectedly, while you are doing easy, relaxed, uncomplicated things: walking, being in nature, waking up from your dreams, journaling, reading, listening to music, simply showing up to where you are and what you are doing, without attachment to any particular idea about how it should or should not be.

When you let go of your attachment to how things should be, or must be . . . this is when you begin to hear Divine messages, which you will recognize as your soul's truth.

How is it, then, that you begin this practice of listening for the sweet whisper of the Universe? How do you begin to learn how to hear this messaging?

The answer is simple, and it can be terrifying.

You simply begin.

You step apart from all the illusion, Misbelief, and group thought of the dominant culture, of your family, of your friends, and you begin to walk your own soul path.

You begin to live your true life, whatever this is for you. And as you step into your true self, you enter in with heart wide open, trusting that all messages will arrive.

In truth, messages are always available to you in every moment! As your ability to enter into stillness, to listen, and to understand what Divine language sounds like expands you will begin to hear messages frequently, if not all the time.

Begin to listen now. Trust that with repeated practice of entering Divine space, you will open, and you will hear.

Consider a question that you'd like to ask the Universe. Close your eyes, breathe, and relax. You will hear a message in your mind instantaneously, even before you can think. Sometimes it arrives very quickly, so quickly you may not realize you have already received it. It may sound like your own voice in your head, but it is not: it is Source. How does this message inform you?

Guidance Arrives in Feeling

The heart is where the soul resides. We have said this to you several times already. Do you begin to understand what it means?

The Universe speaks to you in feeling.

The Universe listens to and answers the call of your heart, and the Universe communicates this response to you in feeling.

When you live in transparency, with full awareness and expression of your heart's feeling, you begin to understand what it is to be free.

So many of you live with hidden hearts!
So many of you live with armored hearts!

So many of you live in fear that if you allow even the slightest piece of Light in, your hearts will shatter into a million pieces.

This is not so.

To live numb to your feelings, to deliberately numb out or hide your feelings . . . this is the greatest tragedy.

Pain felt in the hidden heart is absolute pain. And in an instant, it can be alleviated, opened, and healed with Light. Crack open your heart even the smallest amount, the tiniest sliver, and Light will find its way in.

> *The Universe listens to and answers the call of your heart.*

This is your life, and you can find your way now or you can find your way later, or you can find your way in a next life or lifetimes after that.

But oh, what if you were to crack open your heart NOW, and begin to live in Light?

And if your heart is open now, what if you were to expand it further? Further still? Beyond what you thought was even possible for you?

The Universe communicates to you in your emotions and feelings, and thus, every feeling is a marker of your soul's truth.

If you are being abused and you have the feeling of pain, don't numb it, don't disregard it, don't be afraid of your future! Know and receive this as full information of the Universe guiding you to abandon your abuser, to abandon your role as victim, and live a new way.

If meeting someone causes you anxiety, don't talk yourself out of your feeling. Know and receive this as information from the Universe; the Universe guides you to pay attention, and to see beyond the false front that this person presents.

If you are doing a job and you're feeling depressed, stuck, wasteful, don't fear quitting. It is easy to fear because of the illusions of money, of society, of what everyone else says! Pay attention to this information the Universe brings you in your feeling, and begin to make plans to do something different. When the time is right, the Universe will create new opportunities for you.

For most of you, feelings provide the clearest conveyance of Universal messaging.

Don't deny this steady stream of information by distracting, numbing, resisting. Especially, watch for the slippery, silky way that Misbeliefs, group thought, pressures of the dominant society get in the way, asking you to disregard your feelings.

Don't disregard!

Your feelings are clear messages from the Universe. When you listen to your heart; when you open to what your heart really, truly feels and follow this guidance, you will walk on your soul's path.

It takes courage to follow your soul's path the first time, outside of what others think or tell you to do.

This first step on your own path is how you begin to live from your soul.

When you receive guidance, do you follow it? When you receive visions and messages, do you act on them? Receiving is only the first step. Is there guidance you've received that you know in your heart is true—but that you've been afraid or resistant to follow?

Guidance Arrives in Events

When things change in your life, please pay attention!

A sudden shift in the patterning of your life is one of the ways the Universe communicates with you.

Sometimes, this seems to happen "out of the blue." Even with all your attention to signs, synchronicities, strands . . . you seem to "miss" what is happening as it happens.

And then . . . it just shows up.

Sometimes this shift can be enormously enjoyable and exhilarating: the seemingly instantaneous success of a project, the meeting of a new love, an invitation to travel, and so forth.

This is the best aspect of Flow: when you are sailing along your perfect river, letting the Universe lead you, not worried about anything, just doing your dharma . . . and then something fabulous, wonderful, amazing happens! You experience what is *beyond* your wildest dreams. You experience what answers the calling of your inner heart, and then *expands* upon that. That *overdelivers* the vision you have been working toward, moving toward for all these days, months, even years.

These are wonderful times, worthy of celebration!

You are shown that you can trust the Universe; you are shown this from your own experience. That when you leap, the net will appear. And this encourages you to leap yet again and again, leaving fear behind and living a life of continued expansion and Flow.

However . . .

There are also times when sudden shifts come that do not initially seem positive in nature.

Sudden illness, loss of a job, loss of finances, death of a loved one, loss of relationship . . . these life events knock us off balance, sending us spiraling down into grief and pain and fear.

These events, also guidance from a benevolent Universe, are not so easy to swallow.

Remember: you are here for soul growth. You are here for connection, expansion, love. You are here to become transcendent in God. There is no other purpose.

Thus, if on your chosen human track or path, you are not making progress at the rate that you are ready for, the Universe may step in and guide you, nudge you, propel you onto your path of highest possibility.

Sometimes your life events are joyous, sometimes difficult. But always, whether "good" or "bad," they serve to wake you up. They pull you out of complacency, stuckness, stubbornness, fear, and invite you to open your heart to its fullest capacity.

Thus, when an event "happens" to you out of nowhere, unexpected even when you have been following signs and synchronicities, pay attention! When you experience an event, understand it is the Universe guiding you in a very direct way!

An event may be seen as the Universe communicating directly with you, by shifting the course of your destiny, disrupting the previous pattern of your life so that you may move forward more quickly in the process of your soul growth. Seek to gain understanding from the changes that this event brings.

This is often forgotten when the event is joyous. It is even more difficult to gain this detachment when the event is painful or stressful.

Look at your life as a continuum: this lifetime, that lifetime, the next lifetime . . . all of your lifetimes, in which you are given opportunity to work on your soul growth. Surely, you would not expect a soul seeking expansion to go hide out where it is safe, secure, where nothing happens and nothing changes? As a living being, the only thing you are capable of is change!

Don't hide in your life. Live it. Take risks, let go of the past, move forward, connect, and live in joy.

When there is no joy in a moment, open your heart to what is.

When the Universe guides you with events, trust you are being realigned or repositioned into situations and relationships and understandings that will further your expansion as soul.

Is there a recent event that surprised you, startled you, or brought you into deep awareness of yourself as a soul? Was there a message for you in this event? Did you change your course of action after this event or synchronicity occurred?

> *When there
> is no joy in a
> moment, open
> your heart
> to what is.*

Receiving Creates More Receiving

Remember that you are switching paradigms.

You are moving from the old reality of your dominant culture: fear, pain, numbness, and all the Universes they inhabit: political rule, corporate rule, cultural rule.

You are moving into the new paradigm of intuition, expansion, Oneness, Nowness.

It is not just an entirely different way of living, it is an entirely different way of experiencing your life!

At the beginning, when you are switching from numbness to consciousness, you will have moments where you don't trust the new paradigm. You get sucked back into the old way, the old thought, the pervasive culture of pain and fear that you have become so accustomed to.

Remember: all of this is Misbelief.

What is true, what is real, is that you are free.
You are Divine soul; you are more than your human container.

And when you begin to live in this way—when you begin to live from your soul, rather than from your human aspect—you begin to experience more and more of this freedom.

There is no turning back once you taste this! And, you are not meant to turn back; it is why you are born into this life: to see how far you can get on your path to enlightenment, true consciousness. This is the goal of soul growth.

To become free from all Misbeliefs, pain, and fear.
To move beyond suffering.
To transmute all experiences into love.

At the beginning, it is complicated. You hang on to the cliff with your fingernails, terrified to drop into the net of the Universe, while at the same time longing to let go of all these Misbeliefs that you have been raised with, that you have chosen to believe.

You may hang on to the cliff for years, decades even. In some cases, some souls can't let go of their Misbeliefs in a lifetime, or for lifetimes. These are the unconscious beings you see in pain: creating war, creating violence, creating the suffering that mirrors their own.

And yet, there is another way: to see clearly that what society tells you is not so. And to begin walking on your own path, toward what is true.

As you begin this journey as spiritual psychic, as mystic, as lover, as seeker, as saint; in all the many, many ways you can walk your spiritual path, you will be tempted to look back, to cling again to the old ways.

You don't need to look back.

> *The more you receive the Light, the more radiant you become.*

Step into Divine waters, and step in again. Step in over and over and over. Every time you enter into this immersion of higher vibration and pure love, you are changed.

This baptism, this vibrational immersion, this shifting of your frequency and your understanding, makes it easier and easier to remain in the Light.

The more you receive the Light, the more radiant you become. The more you follow the Light, the easier it is to follow the Light.

In this way, we guide you: seek the Light, follow the Light . . . shun the dark, let go of what is dark.
In this way, you will make your way faster and further, toward the expansion of yourself.

Is there any reason you are afraid of committing to the Divine? Do you understand that the true reality is Light, and more Light, and more Light after that? And that to step into this reality all you have to do is connect, and connect again, and yet again?

On the River of Life

In a recent meditation I had a startlingly strong vision of myself on a wide, flat river, the kind you might see in India. Everything surrounding me was flat and dry: nothing except the bare land, the vast, open sky, and the wide, still river.

I must add, I have been to this river many times in meditation. Perhaps you have too?

In my meditation I was standing on a raft in the middle of the river, and both sides of the raft were attached to ropes on shore, so I could not be pushed forward by the current. There were guides on each bank of the river shouting to me to pay attention. I held a long pole in my hand, to help me keep my balance.

"Pay attention," they cried. "Continue on!"

Yet even as I turned to face forward, I realized that I was actually facing backward. I was actually facing the past.

And as I realized this, the river, which had once appeared to be so still, now rushed forward with a ferocious current.

Struggling to stay upright, I realized that this was the past rushing forward: not just all my experiences in this life and in lifetimes before, but everyone's.

Our collective past. The past of our collective soul.

And the more I tried to keep my position in the rushing, fierce current, the more I lost my footing, the more I struggled.

Suddenly the raft rocked and bucked and with a great creak broke free of the ropes, and I was sailing down the river, my guides laughing and waving to me.

"Let go," they cried. "Continue on!"

The more we struggle with our past: recalling the old wounds, the old hurts once again . . . the more we realize it's futile.

The past is never still, just like the present is never still. We are always flowing to our next Now.

If you're struggling to keep your balance with all your past wounds, just let it go.

The past is over, and you don't have to go there again.

Let it all go, and let the river of life take you to your next Now.

PART NINE

Divine Opening

Scattering of Ashes

The box that held my father's ashes did not contain who he was.

How can you say enough about a person who was your biggest ally, your truest mentor, who believed you were the moon and stars?

It's impossible to sum up a life.

But it is possible to pay homage.

Carrying the box, I made my way down to the beach where my father and I had walked so many summers. Puget Sound is vast: a gentle body of salt water that surrounds the islands north of Washington and joins the Pacific.

Far down the shore, a single heron observed me.

Otherwise, there was no one else around.

I made my way to where the clay cliffs rose from the ground, beside a particular jutting marker, and began to dig a hole in the sand. How big is big enough? I had no idea. Then I opened the box, steeling myself for the reality of it: the grit, the bone, and the fine dust.

How could this be my father?

I thought about him in love, and I did not cry as I poured the ashes into the hollow, covering them with sand. I was still not crying as I turned my gaze out to the sea, praying in love and thanks.

And then I looked up.

There sat an eagle above on the cliff, perched upon a scraggly pine.

Thirty feet up. Maybe less.

Watching me.

He bent his huge white head and stared at me with his eagle eyes, and I knew it was my father.

We remained like this a very long while: the eagle craning his head down, me craning my head up, and I stared at my father while tears poured down my cheeks, and the Universe poured down its love.

Finally, he took one last look, and then in a sudden sublime motion he opened his wings in slow motion, six-foot span spread wide, and he rose up and flew straight toward the sun.

I had to stop crying then, because I was too busy catching my breath.

How Meditation Opens You

Meditation is intentional stillness.

When you meditate, you create a portal into Universal knowledge. This portal is created when you meditate for hours, or just for a few minutes.

In other words, meditation is the portal that allows you to enter into another layer or level of the Universe; it allows you to experience other dimensions beyond your normal human reality.

There are many terms for this. We simply say "entering in."

When you enter in, you access a higher vibrational dimension. This vibration shifts and changes you. It realigns you, heals you, sorts you out. It reverberates with your true nature, which is soul.

Every time you meditate, you remember who you really are.

Every time you meditate, you experience yourself as soul.

Meditation removes you from the distractions of your daily life. For example, when you close your eyes or see with a soft gaze, you remove yourself from visual distractions; closing your eyes allows you to go into an inner space, where you can receive visions in your mind's eye.

When you sit in a quiet space, you remove yourself from the cacophony, the sounds that distract. Removing outer noise allows you to better receive messages in your mind's ear.

When you meditate in nature you immerse yourselves in vibrational frequencies that are whole and balanced; they provide your human form with resonance it can follow and pattern upon, and this is useful and healing for the entire organism.

If you seek guidance from your meditation, most of your guidance will arrive in the first moments after entering in.

This is because when you pose a question to the Universe, it is not a new question: the Universe hears your heart even before you do. Thus, information arrives to you instantaneously: as soon as the question is thought, the answer has arrived.

Your answer is instantaneous. In fact, it sometimes arrives so quickly, you may think you have not received it. You may wait for it, when in fact, it has already arrived.

Every time you meditate, you remember who you really are.

More correctly, the question is always known, and the answer is always known; we will discuss this more later.

For now, understand that visions and messages and knowings arrive to you immediately, from the moment you enter into Divine space. In this way, you can use meditation not only as a method of healing and as a way to experience a prolonged immersion in bliss, but as an instantaneous way to receive guidance from the Universe.

Again: your answers will arrive as soon as you enter in. It is like opening a box and the present is inside; there is no waiting period for the gift to materialize. It is there already. It was there before you opened the box!

You may certainly choose to meditate for longer periods of time, in a formal way, using formal systems. This is a beautiful way to sustain an immersion in Divine frequency.

However, if this is not something that suits you at this time, you will find it beneficial to do the short meditation practice: to sit in stillness, to close your eyes, to breathe, and to ask the questions in your heart. And then, to wait in stillness, eyes closed, as the visions and messages and knowings arrive.

This is enough, for now.

As you begin to settle into this new way, you can expand your time in stillness. Go to your comfort level; don't set a timer, don't keep a watch. Just allow yourself to take the time you need:

a little on some days, a lot on others. You will know exactly what is right for you, in that moment.

We also suggest, at the beginning, do not meditate in a group, or as part of a system. Walk your own path into stillness. Remember it is your soul journey! There are many, many things that you will not understand, until you have the courage to do them by yourself, in your own way. Not following anyone, but following your soul's own understanding.

Go into stillness by yourself; ask your own questions; receive your own guidance.

Later, when you are more in tune with your soul self, you might meditate with others, try other practices. But for now, allow yourself to enter stillness in solitude, so you can become acquainted with the longings of your own heart.

When you enter intentional stillness, you become one with the Universe. There is no time here, no space, only collective awareness, which is God/Divine/One/All. There is no wrong way to do this. Simply close your eyes, breathe, and relax. Allow the Universe to become known within.

How Nature Opens You

When you are in the frequencies of nature, your human container is realigned.

Do you remember how it is with the simplest acts of entering in: how by just closing your eyes, and breathing in through your nose and out through your mouth, you release yourself from the distractions of the world and go within?

This is what spirit requires, your soul being.

But do not forget, you are both at once: soul in human container.

The human container has different requirements. It does not need to fly in the etheric frequencies, to expand and to dissolve into everything all at once, all the time.

Instead, the human container requires the nourishment of its earth self, and it does this by being with others of the same element. By this, we mean the plants, the animals, the minerals, the weather systems, all that is in the natural world.

The natural environment creates an energy vibration very different than the man-made environment, the industrial environment, the computer environment. The man-made frequencies are at once gritty, dull, debilitating, exhausting, sticky, base, buzzy, and upsetting; they are not a match for the human body.

But nature's frequencies are slower, more sustained; they are nurturing, they bring sustenance to the human container. The diffuse mix of all the creatures, plant life, and other aspects of the natural world soothe the human body.

When you sit in nature, regardless if you are at the beach, at the desert, in the woods, by a lake, in all the different ways that nature can show up: you find yourself coming back to yourself. You find yourself breathing more deeply, slowing down, and paying attention to the great wealth and variety of aspect that the natural world contains. You go within, and you forget the thoughts that roamed and scattered even as you thought them in their fast and fragmented way.

Instead, it becomes enough to simply gaze at a leaf, or a burbling stream, or a tree, or the sky, or a rock . . . and to simply experience the moment in gazing at, listening to, being with the natural world.

Your head clears, your body relaxes, what was confusing becomes clear, and anger and anxiety simply dissipate into the gentler, richer rhythms and vibrations of nature.

So many of you live in urban environments, and we say, this alone is not enough to sustain your human container. When you live only surrounded by other human bodies, buildings, machines, and computers: this vibration cannot sustain you in the way you are meant to be sustained. Even one flower, one plant, one animal can change the environment in a room. This extends to the mineral world: the rocks, the crystals, and so forth.

Nature realigns, heals, and comforts your human container.

Nature settles you into trance state by calming the frequencies of your body; when you add into this the intention of entering in while you are in nature, the resulting shift in energy for both body and soul are astounding!

If you do not have easy access to nature, try to bring it into your life so you can still find the energy frequencies that support and nourish your essential human form at the highest level.

In this world, it is common to go without nature for long periods of time: when you work in an urban environment, when you work inside, when you live in places that are shut or closed from the weather system, when you drive in cars; in these cases you are away from nature for long periods of time, even for most or all of the day.

Sometimes, you go your entire day, with only the briefest moment of nature, weather, outdoors. From home to car to work and back again!

We say, nature is not a preference or an option: it is an essential requirement for your human container.

You cannot get what you need, in terms of alignment and entrainment, except from nature.

You cannot reach joy state in a sustained way, unless you are familiar with nature and you dip into it frequently: by this we mean every day.

If you say you do not have time: this is not true.

In every moment, you can take yourself outside, you can take yourself into the unsheltered environment where your own shelter is that of the sky, and you can look up and see what is there: stars, clouds, rain, snow, sun, light.

You can take yourself outside, and you can feel what is on your skin: the air, breath of nature.

You can take yourself outside, and you can notice the trees, even if it is only one tree, battered, on an urban sidewalk. Even this tree: it holds the vibration you seek.

Nature provides an exquisite mix of harmonious collective frequencies that include sound, sight, feeling, and energy as a vibration.

You notice this easily, because even a moment in nature engages you: you become fully connected to Oneness, the moment you take even one moment and pay attention to nature.

In one moment, even in the space of a few seconds, you become engaged by the frequency of nature: by the whispers, sounds, breath of plant, vibration of mineral, by all that is there.

You quickly become entranced by this vibration. It is impossible to resist! So much to notice—so much that is outside of you that you become busy with your noticing, and then you notice that it is not outside of you: that you are part of nature.

Finally, you become entrained to this vibrational state: able to re-create it more quickly when you are in natural surroundings and then, later still, even when you have just a piece of nature to connect to.

> *Nature brings recognition of the true self.*

You become able to meditate upon a stone, whether this stone is in a forest or it is on your office desk. You become able to become one with a leaf, whether this leaf is on a tree or on a plant on your desk.

The vibration of the natural world is the same, wherever you find it.

Slower, quieter, more stable, more still.
More complex, less complex, different.
Brimming with emotion and feeling and awe!

If you become attuned to listening well enough, you begin to understand the visions and the messages and the knowing that nature brings.

Recall: Nature is not separate from your human self. You are also nature. You are a part of it, just as you are a part of everything. You are a natural being, and you belong in the natural world.

When you are in nature, in relaxed state, and you begin to pay attention to the whisperings of the trees, the breath of the wind, the dance of the leaves, the shimmering grace of the mineral world, the quiet observation of the animal and insect kingdom, you recall once again who you really are: soul in body.

The wind speaks to you with clearing breath.
The birds sing to you, and you understand their song.
The trees rustle their leaves in affection to you.
Sit with your back to a tree, and you feel its embrace.
Become very still, and notice a wild creature, and understand that you notice this creature, because you have become the creature.

Your soul knows this well. Your body also knows it. Nature brings recognition of the true self.

Nature teaches Oneness in body. This is one of the most valuable ways you can walk the path of the spiritual psychic: to be in nature, and to communicate with nature, and to become all aspects of nature; to dissolve into it, to disappear into it, to know the bliss of Oneness in this gentle, embodied frequency.

Find the nearest living thing: a plant, a flower, a tree. Meditate upon this plant or flower or tree, with eyes closed or eyes open, until you find you are meditating with it. Notice how differently you feel. Notice how you feel connected in a different way.

How Music Opens You

Music is frequency expressed as sound.

Music is energy with the ability to create resonance in the human container; the frequency of music (and, to be clear, all sound) creates a reaction in the body.

In other words, music shifts frequency in the body.

Recall that nature shifts frequency in the body to make us calmer, more stable, more still, both more complex and less complex, enhancing our sense of Oneness, and expanding our sense of awe.

However, music shifts the frequency in the body so that we are able to feel our emotions.

If the music's frequency does not align with the body, it creates anxiety, fear, anger; it creates discord in the body's energy system.

> *Music shifts the frequency in the body so that we are able to feel our emotions.*

If the music's frequency does align with the body, it creates peace, joy, calm, tranquility, relaxation, healing; it creates resonance in the body's energy system.

Many people study this phenomenon of music, sound, and how it affects the human container.

But most of you just feel it.

In meditation, you recognize yourself as soul. You do this by eliminating the visual cues that distract you with the outer world, by entraining yourself to enter into Divine realm upon the breath: the breath in through the nose, the breath out through the mouth.

In nature, you recognize yourself as human being; the natural self, the animal self, the mortal self, busy in the endless cycle of life, death, and rebirth. You enter into this realm by the diverse and complex visual, auditory, tactile, and energetic vibrations of the natural world around you. These altogether entrance you into entering another layer or level of dimension.

In music, you recognize yourself as heart: this is the emotional self, the feeling self; you are entrained upon the beat, which is irresistible to every human. Your body entrains to rhythm as easily at it entrains to heartbeat when you are in utero. Yet even as the body entrains to beat, the beat and melody entrance further, and transport you to realms where you can access the different dimensions of heart. With music, you feel more: the baser emotions, the higher emotions, the delicious variations in between.

Those who understand this secret about music are able to use it as a tool, a training device, an intoxicant, an enhancer, a cocreator of energy for all the uses of energy, force, and manifestation. When you understand the Divine power of music, you can choose to use it for healing, for expansion, for opening.

It does not matter, anymore, if the music is organic and in person, although this creates a more direct effect. It is true: if you hear a crystal bowl vibrating, you cannot resist the feeling it creates in your body. But because humans now are evolving, music heard via electronica also contains pure energy, vibrational essence.

Consider music: as an intoxicant, enhancer, and tool for entrainment into altered, etheric, and grounded states.

Use music in your life to help you feel your emotions. When you know your emotions, you know your heart. And when you are able to follow your heart, you are always on the right path.

Do an experiment. Switch radio stations between classical, country, rock, hip hop, ambient. Notice how your emotions change, as you are immersed in each style of music. Which music resonates most with how you feel? How you would like to feel?

How Sex Opens You

We are speaking of conscious, transcendent sex.

There are so many other ways to have sex. Not just the unconscious, animal, base, detached sex that is the norm in your society. For this lesson we speak of sex as the highest means of melding and merging in the human body: the closest you can get to another human. The most intimacy, the most connection you can create, between two humans.

Unconscious sex can damage you if you engage in it too early, with the wrong person or people, if you are forced or it is associated with shame, guilt, violence. If you don't approach it wholeheartedly, but engage with body only; not heart, not soul. If you engage from a detached perspective.

These are the ways sex is used to abuse, coerce, and control. These are the ways sex is used in the dominant society to shame. These are the ways sex is experienced as not what it is but as a shameful label—put on what can be the highest of the holy acts, the most sacred of communions.

We say, there is another way to use sex: as a method for opening into Divine space. By this, we mean transcendent sex, created in the energy of love.

There is discussion now in your culture about gender, preference, and so forth as aspects of sexuality. We make no statement on gender.

The soul has no gender.

One does not have the soul of a woman, the soul of a man, the soul of any gender orientation.

Sex does not relate to gender: one man, one woman, and so forth. All genders, all humans, all living beings have sex.

> *In its purest form, sex is a fusion of consciousness.*

This is because in its purest form, sex is a fusion of consciousness.

By fusion we do not mean one plus one. Instead, we mean one plus one plus One: the Divine/One/All/God shows up in the experience, also. The energy of God in the room . . . this is palpable in transcendent sex.

In transcendent sex, the partners connect to each other in the human body, and they also connect to the Divine consciousness of each other. In this fusion they open all emotions, all energy, and all portals to the etheric realms, all at once. Together they enter into Divine vibration via the portal of their bodies and, in this way, they transmute the energy of their human selves into Divine energy.

In conscious sexuality, each person brings not just his or her body to the equation, but also their deepest connection with Divine/One/All.

This is merging beyond the skin. It is merging of the soul, at the highest levels of vibration.

In this way, it is possible for partners to experience aural blending; spontaneous experience of shifts in time/space such as past lives, future lives, bilocation (being in two places simultaneously); spontaneous healing; the palpable sense of Divine energy; and direct knowing.

This is simply what can happen when you choose to become conscious with another person, through transcendent sex.

We say, there is no special technique for this: there is tantra that is ancient, there is technique-based tantra that uses the breath, for example. These ways might create the ecstatic experience, but they do not always contain the heart opening required for true intimacy.

To open the heart to another, in complete vulnerability and in complete surrender to the partnership . . . this is no easy task for the personality, the ego, the human container! And yet, it is this tantra of love, that creates true transcendence. It is what simply happens when two people are vulnerable, intimate and heart open to the fullest expansion, and when they hold space in the Divine together.

The body dissolves away at this point; it is only soul burning with soul, burning with the transfulgent flame of the Divine.

Have you experienced transcendent sex? If you have, can you recall what qualities in you and/or the other person created this conscious connection?

How Peak Experiences
Open You

A peak experience is a moment in which you become exquisitely attuned to the miracle of Now.

It is common to have a sudden experience of Nowness when you are in new settings, doing unfamiliar things: the newness creates a heightened perception of your reality. However, having a peak experience does not require adventure or adrenaline.

Rather, peak experiences are often simple and serendipitous, happening when you least expect them. They are experiences of pure presence, and they may be short, such as a few seconds, or long, such as many hours or even days. In peak experiences, you enter a portal that takes you to the bliss state: one of the most expanded states. And you experience this state fully in the environment: fully embodied, eyes wide open, all senses operating.

Some of the names for this—kundalini opening, bliss, nirvana, and so forth—imply that you must do something to create this state. But, again, a peak experience happens on its own, without you even trying.

It is a matter of moving aside your distractions and simply being in what is.

Thus, there is no place you need to travel to, no drug you need to take, no adventure you need to sign up for, no practice you need to be doing to have a peak experience.

You simply need to show up to your real life, exactly as it is this moment, and be in it fully, with all your perception.

Peak experiences are ordinary moments, perceived in an extraordinary way.

Drop your ego on the floor, and drop your distractions there as well. Enter fully in the Now moment:

To drink a cup of coffee can be a peak experience.
To walk without destination can be a peak experience.
To get up early with the sun can be a peak experience.
To take a shower can be a peak experience.

In this way, you see that peak experiences are ordinary moments, perceived in an extraordinary way.

The question is, how many of these peak experiences are you having in your ordinary day?

For those who live from soul state, the answer would be not just one, or a handful, but many, many moments of these in a day.

These moments are not rare or elusive: when we are conscious, they happen all the time. We shift our perception that life is boring, mundane, ordinary, into understanding the astounding beauty of each moment.

It's as if you suddenly flipped a light switch in your consciousness— in one moment you were distracted, agitated; in mind thought, group thought; out of body in past memory or future projection, and so forth—and then in the next moment you dropped out of all that chaos and into consciousness.

In that moment of Now, you experience everything as it really is: all of it, all at once.

There are practices that can be done to create peak experiences: drugs, adventure, even types of breathwork, and yoga. But we say, come to miracles in a softer way. Let your perception be something that shifts slowly, so that each day you wake up and you find yourself more conscious.

In this way, your own expansion brings you to experiences of presence, which bring you to more expansion and so on.

In this way, by opening slowly, like a flower in the Light, you will begin to change the way you live from distraction to full presence, from illusion to true reality.

Don't force the opening. Allow that the slow opening opens you more completely, over time. You are here to experience peak experiences all the time, in the tiniest aspects of your everyday life. This is the way you can live here on earth, if you so choose.

What's a peak experience that you've had today? If you haven't had a peak experience yet today, can you make some room in your life so that you will? How would you go about trying to create that?

How Stillness Opens You

. . . .

Do you recall how when you meditate, you close your eyes and let your body become still? And in this way of dropping out of distraction, you become more able to enter the etheric portals available to you?

Entering stillness is one way you can easily enter into the other dimensions that heal, inform, and elevate you.

By entering stillness, you are able to more easily open your windows to the Divine.

It is true; you can enter into direct connection with the Divine anywhere: in a car, in a crowd, in a hospital. God is always in the room; there is no time the Universe is not actively listening and responding to your heart's longing.

In this way, the Universe has no trouble hearing you.

However, it is easier for you to understand what the Universe is communicating to you when you drop out of worldly distractions, and when you relax your body.

The Universe hears you at all times.
You are able to hear better, when you drop out of distraction.

The human self enjoys continuous distraction. There is always the new environment, the new person, the new object, the new drug, the new drama, the new experience. This continued grasping of what is bigger, better, newer is how the human self acts before it becomes conscious. This continued grasping or attachment for the next thing or the next experience is addictive; there is no end to it.

In this way, you have an addiction to experience, an addiction to things. And the more you grasp, the more you desire, the more you grasp, and so on. Many people live their lives this way, addicted to distraction, without ever breaking the cycle.

We begin to see that we need to change when we notice that busyness has taken over our lives. When our lives seem to be a continuous list of "to-dos."

When we start to live our schedule, as if it were our life.

Sometimes, in modern life, we confuse this idea of being "busy" with that of being good, or meaningful, or important. As if, the more we can accomplish on our list, the more we are living.

Sometimes, in modern life, we become competitive with our time, as if whoever can be busier is the one who is having a "better" or more important or meaningful life.

And yet, the opposite is true. As both a human being and a soul, as an integrated body-and-spirit being, you are not meant to be "busy" all the time.

The body requires relaxation, downtime, relief from stress, laziness, dreaming, sleep, music, movement, nature, laughter, affection, sex, joy; this is what the body needs to feel good, to be healthy, to be whole.

The soul also requires relaxation, downtime, dreaming, day dreaming, spacing out, creative musing, etheric journeying, emotions, and understanding fully felt and expressed; this is what the soul needs to continue to expand.

When we repress this need to expand ourselves in the body or soul, or both, we get a person who is not complete, not authentic, not living with heart singing.

Even more, we get a person who is stressed, tired, cranky, overly expressed in the outer world, engaged in activities that are not authentic or meaningful. We get a body that wants to drop out, numb out, and resist. And we get a soul that feels a great sense of loss because, in disconnected busyness, we are distracted at all moments from our Divine nature.

Yes, it is possible to become so expanded in your nature that you can plow through a huge schedule of tasks and appointments—a phenomenal level of busyness—and still be in present moment of Now at all times. However, most of us aren't at that level yet!

Most of us can't deal with continued busyness or distraction over time, even though our society tells us we should be able to handle it. If we try anyway . . . the price is too steep.

Being still, or learning to become still, is the first step we must take in order to discover the full extent of our addiction to distraction.

This initial journey into stillness isn't easy: it absolutely brings up tremendous emotion and unease; by taking away all the sensory and emotional load of our distractions, stillness requires that we look at and sit with and feel what we really feel.

Stillness helps us know our truth.

When you find yourself in a very busy life, you can be sure that you have strayed from your soul path. The soul is not here to check off to-do lists. The soul is here to expand, and to understand, and to participate in the Now.

> *You can't get to Now from a to-do list.*

You can't get to Now from a to-do list.

Now arrives, when you are brave enough to see what lies beyond distraction.

How many things are on your schedule today? What would happen if you let go of half of these? More? If you have ten "to-dos" on your schedule, what if you cut out five? Which would you drop first? If you had three "to-dos," what if you pared it down to one? What's the most important? What does't matter at all? Do you understand that it is within your power to create a spacious life? How would your life change, if you started to do this?

You Can Read Anything

When you start to understand how the Universe speaks to you—in visions and messages, events and emotions, nature and music and sex and peak experiences and stillness—you begin to realize something awesome:

The more present you are, the more Universal guidance you receive.

The more present you are, the more clarity you have.

The more present you are, the more you experience direct knowing.

The more you pay attention to what's really going on, not what society tells you, or your family or your culture or the Misbeliefs you were raised with, the more you relax, breathe, and are simply aware of the actual events and feelings and experiences in your life.

> *The more present you are, the more Universal guidance you receive.*

The more you pay attention to the exquisite reality of your life, the more present you become. And when you become truly present, you can "read" anything; you can gather psychic information from anything.

This ability to become so present, so attuned to what is happening right in front of you, allows you to use this understanding to feel, see, predict, or forecast what is being created in Universal Flow.

In other words, by being exquisitely attuned to both your physical and emotional reality, you can understand where you are being guided by the Universe.

By looking at a teacup, you might receive a vision of your next step.
By walking in the woods, you might receive a message of your next step.
By observing an animal, you might understand a difficult situation.
By listening to a piece of music, you might understand how you feel about something.

The heart is where the soul resides.
Direct knowing is revealed to us in the heart.
The heart engages, senses, feels with everything around us and in us.

Thus, by looking at everything, every little and big thing, we can know our soul truth.

We might first learn to do this visually, by using a technique of clairvoyance or spiritual visioning, where we put up a "rose" or other living, animate object in mind's eye, and we observe what this object does in relationship to our asked question. The "rose" itself doesn't matter in any way. It could be anything, and again, it doesn't have to be in the mind's eye.

Anything can be an energetic container in this way.

Because anything and everything is One. We are all part and the sum of Oneness, all at the same time. We are in infinite relationship to each other.

Thus, what is expressed in one aspect of Oneness (what the "rose" does, or what an animal does, or what the weather does, or what a coworker does), all of this relates to your question or query or wondering about your next step.

Everything is connected.
Everything is in relationship to everything else.
Everything is one of One.

We may also, for a moment, choose to create a smaller container of the Universe of One. We may, as easily as we might scoop a cup of water from a pool, scoop out the Universe we wish to look at and observe and sense, from the bigger Universe of All.

And we know, we trust, that it's absolute, that the water in the cup holds and expresses the exact same reality as the water in the pool.

The small reflects the big, because the small is the big.

A piece of Oneness reflects the All of Oneness, because they are the same.

Thus, you can read from anything: you can take any object, living or inanimate; any event; any person; and you can in observation and sensing of this small Universe, perceive the energy of the whole.

And in this way, you might sense the energy of this small Universe, the object, the event, the person, across time and space. You might look at where the small Universe is now and foresee or foretell or have direct knowing of where it is going.

Of course, the ultimate answer is always love.

There is no other answer than this.

But the smaller answer, the answer that is of greatest interest to the human path of the soul-in-human container, is also available.

And, this smaller answer: Where am I headed? What am I doing? Am I in right relationship? Am I doing my right work? What is my life's path? What is my life's purpose? What is my highest expression of my true self? What is my next step?

This smaller answer is easily divulged from observation, sensing, and knowing of the small container of Universal energy.

Thus, you can read anything.

You do not need divination tools that were proscribed in previous ages: pendulum, tarot cards, and so forth. In fact, we say, most of these do not utilize the full aspect of Light. And some, such as ouija, are aspects of dark.

You do not need anything other than your own human container. To connect or raise to the vibration of your soul, all you need to do is close your eyes, or gaze softly with a soft, diffuse gaze, taking everything in all at once, at the particulate level. Breathe in through the nose, out through the mouth until you are relaxed.

In simply sensing, feeling, and becoming one with the object, person, or event you are looking at, and in asking your question, all will be revealed. You will understand, by what you observe, sense, and feel from this object, person, or event, your answer.

This is a new way of being for many of you. Try this, and then continue to try. It takes practice, to enter fully into this way of full presence.

Think of a question that you'd like to ask the Universe. Now, looking around the room or wherever you are, let your eyes come to rest on whatever object you are drawn to. Quietly consider this object. How does it relate symbolically or emotionally to your question?

Everything Is Your Answer

This understanding that the Universe is speaking to you at all times, in all ways . . . this understanding comes to you slowly.

It arrives to you over time, and it arrives to you with the expansion of your consciousness, and it arrives to you with practice.

In the beginning, when you were a child and still open to these things, the Universe spoke to you easily, and you heard without doubt.

When you were young, you spoke the language and you understood the language, and all was clear to you.

You had not yet learned to rely upon language, symbol, and so forth, and thus you felt the Universe; you received the Universe as emotion, feeling, direct knowing.

This mostly happened in the body, for you were connected to your body then in a different way. Your body, as conduit of your emotion and your knowing, connected you to all things: the breath of air on your shoulder, the great stillness of the night, the grasses waving upon your bare legs.

For some, there was more: you saw visions of the future; you saw energy and etheric beings in the room. You saw these clearly, outside of your mind's eye, as apparition. You saw beyond the veil, and the veil was mostly open for you.

Then as you were indoctrinated by the dominant culture, by your schools and family and place of origin, and all the ways that humans are moved away from higher vibration and individual experience into lower vibration and group thought, you began to understand the Universe less.

When the Universe spoke to you in messages and visions, you heard this language; but you began to lose trust. You questioned what you heard.

When the Universe spoke to you with energy and events and synchronicity, you noticed still, but you began to downplay what was happening. You didn't trust, and you didn't follow: you questioned or, worse, you scoffed or called it coincidence or "random."

You forgot that magic is real, and that synchronicities are the way the Universe gets our attention whenever it is trying to nudge us into a new understanding or a new direction.

And then you got busy with all the things a life contains, and you stopped listening entirely. In fact, you forget you knew how to listen!

It took a long time, as you merrily went upon your way, addicted to distraction and doing, for the Universe to get your attention again.

For some of you, it was one big event that you couldn't not pay attention to: illness, job loss, financial ruin, divorce, death. The Universe demanded your attention and, if you were very lucky, you began to remember who you really were. And then, in this opening, this surrendering, this casting out of all the Misbeliefs that you'd been taught to believe, you began to hear it again: the Universe speaking to you.

You felt it in your body.
You saw it in your mind's eye.
You heard it in your mind's ear.
You understood synchronicities for what they are: the Universe suggesting you move in a particular direction.

You began to see signs in all things: a bird on a window sill, the weather system moving in, the mystery of a new moon.

You began to remember, and you began to listen, and the more you listened, the more it all came back: this is a language you know! This is the language you speak! This is your language, because this is what you are!

You can read anything because you understand the language; you knew it when you were young, and you can remember it now.

The answer is in everything, because you are part of everything and everything is part of you.

> *The answer is in everything, because you are part of everything and everything is part of you.*

Look within, look without, look small, look big . . . the answer is in everything because everything is One, and thus everything contains the essence and the answer and the truth of everything else.

Let yourself remember this ancient language that you once knew so well.

Let yourself believe that magic, stardust, infinity, Divinity . . . all this is what you are.

Do you believe that you know the language of the Universe? Does this understanding help you trust the Divine guidance you're always receiving? Does your understanding help you to follow this guidance?

Saying I Love You

The little town of Independence, Oregon, population eighty-seven hundred, sure knows how to show the love on Valentine's Day.

That's because on February 14, every wrought-iron lamp on Main Street is festooned with bright red and pink hearts.

Ken loves Michelle.

Grandma loves Rachel and Justin.

Shawna loves Antonio.

We love Sparky and Mittens!

You get the idea.

For a small fee, anyone who wants to can buy a red heart, and the city makes sure it's posted.

Lots of love, festooned all over town!

Big, loud love, proclaimed for all!

Young love, old love, cats and dogs love!

You know . . . it takes guts to proclaim our love, in front of the whole world, in front of our community, even in front of each other.

We might mumble, "I love you" on the phone, or say it in a distracted way as we're headed out the door, or with a sleepy goodnight kiss, tucking our child into bed.

We all love . . . but the proclaiming? That's where it can get sticky.

Some of us say it easily.

Some of us are shy.

Some of us find it difficult, as if our hearts might crack into pieces.

Some of us can't say it at all.

Some of us can say it and mean it, with our whole hearts open.

If you find it difficult to say "I love you" to the people in your life, practice saying it in your meditation, in your prayer, on your walks, in yoga class, in your journal, right before you fall asleep.

Start getting that steady stream of love going in your mind.

You will be astounded at how you start to feel.

You will be amazed at your capacity for love.

PART TEN

Direct Knowing

The Brown Cabinet

There's a particular import store in Portland that always gives me the chills.

I step in, and I'm flooded with impressions from all the artifacts and antiques from other lands: India, Mexico, Peru, Japan, China. From dishes to prayer rugs to family photos from generations past, it's all there.

It all comes in at once: the stories of all these people from all these other places, seeping into your skin. The upstairs of the warehouse is vibrant: colorful and decorated, with lively music playing. But the downstairs is almost spooky: a depository of antique furniture, settled there for years and years.

Including my brown cabinet.

I first spotted it almost a decade ago, and it's still there: the brown healer's chest from China that's so familiar to me that I wonder if it was once mine in a past life. Eight years ago, I walked straight to this chest the first time I entered the store. I was drawn to it like a magnet: up the street, through the doors, down the stairs, all the way to the far wall behind a stack of red lacquered chairs from whence it called.

My hair stood on end when I first saw it: on my head, on my arms. I felt woozy, like I might collapse.

Everything was known to me of this beloved chest! The dark wood, burnished over time. The drawers, six across and six down, once used to hold medicine and herbs. The way the drawers weren't single, but had a secret compartment behind each one; something only the owner would know. Seventy-two spaces total; a plethora of healing.

When I close my eyes, the memory returns: I am standing beside this cabinet, pulling out packets of herbs for the villagers who arrive, one after another at my door. I do this all day long, my whole life, in a one-room hut in ancient China.

Is this memory? Is this past life? Can we really see beyond the layers and levels of this reality? This happens all the time to so many of us. We've all experienced our own version of the brown chest: when we know what we can't possibly know. This is yet another reminder of our infinite selves.

Radical Releasing

The simplest way for you to live as your true Self is to release what you are not.

We say, one reason you don't remember your true nature is that you have collected so many Misbeliefs over time.

These Misbeliefs cloud your understanding.

What are they? Misbeliefs are beliefs, belief systems, ways of looking at the world, and thoughts about yourself and others that are incorrect, that do not reflect your true nature.

Usually, Misbeliefs are imprinted on you by the dominant culture: your family, group thought, and so forth. Sometimes, you form them through experiences that you've misinterpreted or not yet integrated.

The truth is this: You are a Divine being, your essence is Divine, and you are Divine in all ways. You are blessed, beautiful, and loved in all ways and all times. However, because you are contained in human form, your growth and understanding is expressed in human ways. By this, we mean your heart.

Again, we say, the heart is where the soul resides.

Thus, all of your spiritual understanding, all of your soul growth must take place in your human heart. By heart, we don't mean the physical structure. We mean your emotions, your feelings, your understanding, and your willingness to open toward the Light.

To achieve this freedom, this expansion, this Lightness in the heart, you must first clear the grey and dark energies of Misbeliefs. Clearing Misbeliefs does not require special techniques and does not take a long time. All that is required is a radical releasing of all wounding, hurt, anger, fear.

This is done first by recognizing the Misbeliefs you carry, and then by simply determining that you wish to become free. You do not need to experience the full process of healing to become free. Simply hold the intention of freedom.

As soon as you wish to become free, you are.

> *As soon as you wish to become free, you are.*

Again, the process of revealing hidden wounds and processing those wounds is one way to become free over time. But you can also simply work in Light, and create the intention to let Light into your heart.

In our world, everything is instantaneous; you may also enjoy instantaneous healing, which you call miracles. In this way, you may choose to allow a radical releasing of all old Misbeliefs, and in allowing this releasing and clearing from the Divine, Light will pour in so quickly and with such blazing radiance, all darkness will be no more.

This is radical releasing: an instantaneous and direct transmission of the Light, by which all darkness is instantly removed.

You can do this with Misbeliefs, old thoughts, old patterns, old wounds.

You can also do this with disease in the body.

Radical releasing is the intention of becoming free from all darkness, instantaneously and wholly. It is the desire to release all that you are not: the lower energies, the wounding, the hurt, the pain, the fear, the distraction, and so forth.

And of course, because everything is Now, because all is One, this is accomplished instantaneously, simply upon the moment of your intention, wish, or asking.

If you wish to become free, create intention for radical releasing of all that is not you, all that is not Light.

Thus, you become free to experience your true essence.

What would you like to release right now? Is there something that you don't need any longer, that doesn't work for you any longer? Something from your past, that is no longer "you"? When you are ready, ask the Universe to release this now.

Radical Compassion

In radical compassion, you have extreme and total understanding of the other as yourself.

You have complete cognizance of yourself and others as One.

You realize that there is no separation, ever. You realize that what happens to the least of you, happens to All. You realize that your own soul, the collective soul, and the ineffable energy of God/One/All is the same, and that this same is true for the soul of every other being.

There is no them. It is all us.

With this understanding, you begin to shift your behaviors to match this new, conscious way you see the world.

You begin to see the pain in all beings, and you want to alleviate suffering.

You begin to see the confusion of many beings, and you want to help.

You begin to see that others, regardless of how strong or perfect they appear, all suffer in the same way, with the same pains and confusion, and you feel compassion.

In radical compassion, you walk in the world with the greatest empathy and also hold the greatest Light.

Radical compassion does not mean you try to "fix" all you see. You don't try to save them. Truly, it is not yours to save other souls: each soul must do this for themselves.

But it is yours to shine a Light, so that others may see it, and use it as a guide out of darkness and misery.

When you show up in the world in radical compassion, you show up with both extreme empathy and extraordinary joy.

You bring the full depth of your understanding to another's pain, and you acknowledge this pain, and you feel it in your own heart.

You witness it. You know it as your own, because you are One.

There is no them. It is all us.

And in that same moment, you transmute this pain into Light: you bring the ability of your own heart to experience Light, and you shine your radiant heart so that the other may see and know that this is possible for him or her as well.

You feel the pain with empathy.
You transmute the pain with Light.

This is not a healing; it is not going out and trying to lift up or save or heal another. It is just simply what happens, when you walk in the world in this way.

It is normal to desire to walk in the world in this way, with Light blazing from heart, and still not be able to do this all of the time. To get tripped up on your experience of pain, to become so empathetic that you take on other's wounds, and in that experience of suffering, to forget that you know the way to Light.

Sometimes, when you seek to hold compassion, you get tripped up on all that pain . . . you lash out, you get angry, you get sad, you get depressed, and so forth. It all seems too much, this world with all of its pain. Do not be disheartened. Keep leaning toward the Light.

There are many souls here, on many different stages of the path. Keep leaning toward the Light, keep opening to it, keep blazing it forth.

In time, this will become simple for you. In time, you will learn to transmute pain into Light, easily, wherever you are.

Do you believe it is necessary to take on another's pain to alleviate their suffering? Or is there another way to help a person who is suffering? Recall the times you've taken on another's pain, and how that worked. Then, recall the times you simply were present, holding the Light of love and compassion.

Radical Gratitude

•◦•

When you start to have awareness, you begin to experience miracles.

You begin to see that miracles are just how life works; that every "coincidence" or sign or synchronicity is the convergence of the Universe and all its souls and energies working to move you and all souls and energies forward into the greater energy of love.

You're swimming in a river of love!

There is no time this isn't true!

All that love, buoying you up, carrying you, immersing you, baptizing you, moving you forward to the next experience, the next experience, the next . . . this is the true reality.

As spirit, in your soul Self, you know this completely.

As human, in your body, in your every day, with the particular characteristics of your personality, and the Misbeliefs and group thought and lower energies that surround you at every juncture, it is harder to know this.

You're swimming in a river of love!

This is the journey of your soul-in-human-body: to see the illusion, the dream, the maya of the human world. To understand your true reality as spirit, and to know this spirit Self as love.

And the delicious part is this: you get to do all of this within the exquisite richness of the human heart, the human emotions, the extraordinary way your human self is able to feel in the body, and in the emotional body.

Your spirit self does not feel this way; it is all etheric Light!

Yet your human self: here are all the riches of a body experiencing everything, of relationships with other embodied souls, and of the extraordinary energy of emotions, and of the personality itself! The personality itself, with all its flaws and foibles, moving toward greater understanding, leaning toward Light!

Without your human form, there would be nothing for you to learn, nothing to experience, no way to grow.

This is the greatest gift, to have this experience, this soul journey in human form!

A soul cannot see a glorious sunset.

A soul cannot hear the whisper of nature.

A soul cannot hug someone, or hold someone's hand.

A soul cannot know the greatest comforts of home.

A soul cannot experience the gift of sacred sex.

A soul cannot experience the birth of a child.

A soul cannot experience love of the Beloved over time.

A soul cannot enjoy family, friends, and love over time.

A soul cannot try and learn, and try and learn again.

A soul cannot enjoy the passion of a life's work.

A soul cannot experience the ultimate surrender in death.

All of these beautiful, wondrous, amazing, heart-opening experiences are received and enjoyed and experienced in the human body.

Souls are perfect, etheric energy without form. But in the human container, the heart is where the soul feels everything.

The heart is where you feel all the miracles that are good, that open you to more heart opening. The heart is where you feel all the miracles that are "bad," that also open you to shift, change, and grow.

We say, it is a gift to be human, to have these experiences, to learn and love and grow with each other!

Radical gratitude, the saying of a thousand thank yous . . . this is the response of all souls when they return from a lifetime.

Radical gratitude, for the good, the bad . . . the all of it. This is the response of all souls, when they return from a lifetime.

Radical gratitude: to be there, to see it all, experience it all, heart opening, and opening even further than you thought possible.

Move toward this heart opening in your life. There is no other direction that will take you further, make you happier, or bring you more Light.

Make a list of all the beautiful parts of your human life that you appreciate and enjoy. When you are done, spend some time in gratitude for this amazing miracle that is your life.

Radical Intuition

* *

When you start to pay attention, there's nothing you can't know.

This is because intuition comes from consciousness.

Do you remember how we spoke of the two-fold path? The idea that when you journey on the spiritual path your intuitive abilities open fully. And when you journey on the intuitive path, your spiritual self opens. And that these are the self-same paths, walked from different directions?

When you work on spiritual practices that create consciousness— when you meditate, pray, rest, relax, become mindful, become intentional, appreciate, and allow yourself full feeling from an ever-opening heart—you also find yourself becoming psychic.

It is true, you can learn psychic tricks without the accompanying grace of consciousness; however, this will not move you forward on your soul path; it is a false path that leads to nowhere.

Instead, wander the earth in full appreciation for what is, in full mindful greeting of this moment, and the next moment, and the next, in a state of radical gratitude for all that you are experiencing as soul in human container. . . .

The natural progression of this spirit-led, heart-open way of being is connection with All.

As you open your heart, you become fully connected with everything: all creatures, beings, energies, entities, matters, dimensions, the all of it. You experience this connection in your heart, and as your heart connects to All, it opens yet again—expansion bringing more expansion—until your entire heart is cracked open into the extraordinary radiance of pure Light!

How can you not, in this state of vibration, be one of One? How can you not, in this state of vibration, know yourself as Divine?

And, of course, as a small Universe of One, you know everything that has happened, is happening, will happen in the larger Universe of One.

One of the reasons you get confused here is because most of you are not able to retain the splendid vibration of Light for very long. You glimpse Oneness. You have a moment of connection with All-that-is. You stay in this vibration for a moment, and you see the beauty!

Intuition comes from consciousness.

We say, it is this exquisite beauty that we see always, in you and around you. However, because you are still learning as a being, you are unable to hold that vibrational state. You slide back down into a lower, more familiar vibration, and there you are once again . . . walking in the mystery.

You enter in, you connect with All.
You enter in, you receive all knowing of All (what you call "psychic").
You enter in, and you know yourself as soul, and all around you as collective soul.

And then, the vibrations become too high for you. This is normal. Your soul is etheric, but your body is created in human form.

It takes time and practice and intention to learn how to hold the vibration of the etheric world. When you work with us, with guides and the angelic realm, we hold the vibration for you.

Regardless, it takes time to breathe easily in this atmosphere!

If you seek to enjoy radical intuition, continue on your path of opening, being, entering in. As you move intentionally toward a more conscious way of living, your intuition, your psychic self, opens as well.

You cannot stop this. These paths, spiritual and intuitive, are one and the same.

Pose a question to the Universe. This could be something your'e working on right now, or something that you've been pondering for a very long time. Choose the question that arrives effortlessly into your mind. Now, enter into a state of high vibration, in whatever way you like: deep breathing, relaxing, laughter. Do you notice how the answer to your question arrives immediately, the moment you reach a state of bliss?

LESSON 58

Direct Knowing

Intuition is the foreseeing and the foretelling; it is the sensing of energy, the knowing when something is different in the energy of the Universe at a particular time, because you are conscious.

Direct knowing takes things further.

In direct knowing, you have become so attuned to the subtle shiftings and whispers of the Universe, you don't even sense them as something outside of yourself anymore; you don't even sense them as intuition.

Instead you know everything all at once.

For example, if you wish to determine which way the wind is blowing, you might hold a finger up to the air.

If you wish to determine your direction, you might look to the stars and see where the constellations are in the sky.

If you wish to soothe a crying baby, you might hold the baby to your heart, and communicate with it telepathically.

These are ways you use intuition, as the inevitable outcome of your conscious nature, of the Oneness of your being.

And yet in direct knowing, there is more.

It is a dissolving of the Self, the dismantling, the dissolution. As if, for a moment, the you that is you was suddenly not there.

And in this moment you became the other thing, event, time, place, idea. The self you recognized as you simply vanished, and your Oneness shone forth. And in this moment, if you wished to determine which way the wind was blowing, you suddenly felt the wind, and all the winds everywhere for all time, as your Self. You became the wind; you knew it as essence, because it was you.

If you wished to determine your direction, you knew your way without looking to the stars or the constellations, because you recognized yourself as stardust, as star, as constellation, and you knew your place in the Universe, because you were That.

And if you wished to soothe a crying baby, you might find yourself, without warning or thought or intention, simply becoming the idea of hush, or comfort or love, and at the same time becoming One with the baby, so that this Oneness that was you and the baby suddenly became the essence of hush, comfort, love.

In this way, direct knowing might also be understood as direct being.

This is a hard concept for some of you. It is not about losing yourself, or becoming something else. It is about expanding and opening yourself to such great radiance that you simply are all that is.

Direct knowing might also be understood as direct being.

And in this way, the wind, the stars, the baby, you know yourself directly as That. You understand yourself directly as That.

And this direct knowing is true for all things: all in the living and non-living, known and unknown Universe, in all dimensions, forms, and times.

This is what you are.

Direct knowing, is simply the recognition of soul self as That.

Close your eyes, breathe, and connect with the Universe. When you are ready, ask yourself "What is my true essence?" Where do you feel the answer to this question? In your body? Your heart? As an emotion? As a knowing?

Letting the Universe Lead

⟡•◦•◦•◦•◦•◦•◦•◦•◦•◦•◦•◦•◦•◦•◦•◦•◦•◦•◦•⟡

When you let the Universe lead, you exist in Divine Flow.

Thus, you can allow this to happen without fear, without worry or without need to plan and plot and control.

To live in Flow will take you so much further, so much faster, than you might ever create by yourself!

To harness yourself to the power of pure Light, will create in you such greater understanding, such greater joy than what you can build in the constructs of your own human mind. Imagine if you are an ant working on an anthill. And you are taken up suddenly into human perspective, and you see suddenly how big and fast and extraordinary this life experience can be.

Things you cannot even imagine are possible! Things you cannot even comprehend are real! Miracles are the way things are, all the time!

This is what happens when you let the Universe lead. When you put down your goals and your to-do list and your schedules and your plans and simply concentrate instead on having the fullest, richest experience in every moment, at the time that that moment is happening.

Not living in the past.
Not living for the future.
Living right now, fully, richly, exactly as you are in this moment, with exactly what you experience in this moment.

Your only requirement as soul in human form is to concentrate on, pay attention to, and exist fully in the Now.

As you begin to learn how to be in the Now, you are automatically and intrinsically placed at the very center of Flow, the marvelous river of energy that carries you to your next experience. And your next, and your next, each experience broadening and opening and expanding yourself as a being into the greatest understanding and experiencing of Light!

When you let the Universe lead, you allow yourself to let go of control (which is, of course, all illusion), and attach to the true reality of Flow. And in this way, you are automatically brought to experiences that are far greater, bigger, richer than you might have chosen on your own, or that you might have even been able to comprehend or to imagine.

The Universe contains mysteries and miracles that are not in your imagination. And yet, these also are available to you, when you choose to live in Flow.

And what is Flow? Flow is simply the energy of love.

Dream big enough for where the Universe longs to take you. Let go and simply allow this grand gift to be bestowed upon you.

> *What is Flow? Flow is simply the energy of love.*

And, of course, we do not mean dream of a big house, big bank account, big fame, big power . . . all the things dominant society has taught you that you're supposed to want.

Those are hollow success. They will never satisfy. They are the false paths, and they lead endlessly to nowhere.

The real Light is found when you dream big for the things that truly matter: the heart-opening gifts of connection, love, beauty, grace, and awe that you are here to experience in this lifetime, over and over again.

Let the Universe lead. The river of Flow takes you to the greatest joy.

What do you think would happen if you were to lay down all your earthly desires and plans and ambitions, and simply follow the Universe?

Living in Flow

* *

You have become so used to the Misbelief of struggle; you forget that's not how things are.

The Universe is vast, unlimited, infinite energy! All you need to do is accept that you are not separate from this energy, and you become part of it.

The idea of struggle, worry, fear, lack, limit . . . this all stems from the idea that you are separate from, different from, outside of, or kept away from God/One/All.

This is Misbelief, illusion, maya.

You are not separate; you never have been separate, you never will be separate, it is not possible for you to be separate, because you are That Which Is.

Does a tree feel separate from God?

Does a flower?
Does a deer feel separate walking in a meadow?
Does the sun feel separate, apart from God?

No. All of these exist as part of because that is intrinsically what they are.

You are not separate; you never have been separate, you never will be separate.

There is no separation: not for a tree, not for a flower, not for a deer, not for the sun.

Not for you.

For humans, with all their thoughts and egoic concerns . . . the mind loops into lower vibrations, and the mind attaches to lower vibration, and the dominant culture reinforces these thoughts, and suddenly you are in a state of fear, worry, anger, violence, anxiety, and so forth . . . all the lower energies become your reality.

And then you begin to grasp and compete and control and demand . . . even knowing in your soul Self that this is not possible.

It is not possible to grasp the river.
It is not possible to push the river.
The river of Flow is all energy, all Light, only love.

You can't hold it, push it, change it . . . you can only allow yourself to be carried in its currents, letting go of all lower thought, all dominant thought, all the cultural Misbeliefs.

Sometimes the current of Flow is gentle, easy. Other times it's fast and exhilarating. Sometimes the current is slow, meandering. Other times, so wild it's scary. All are ways that the Universe moves you into position, shifts you from your current status quo into the next place or space where you can be most easily reached by Light.

The river of Flow is always changing, just as you know that you are always changing, and the people and events around you are always changing. Trust that change is normal, the way things are, a good thing!

You are always moving forward in this lifetime, toward greater connection, expansion, and love. This is why you're here: for soul growth in this way.

Stop trying to control your experience, and simply live in what is. This is what it means to live in Flow, letting the Universe lead you to Light, and more Light still, and yet again more Light.

If you are not separate from the Universe, which is God/One/ All/Divine, which is the energy of love, then what are you?

Rain

I grew up in Seattle, so let's just say I'm familiar with rain.

We don't use raincoats or umbrellas in Seattle; at least I sure didn't as a kid when I was riding my bike in the misty gloom from the soccer field, or as a teen wandering around downtown drenched in the drizzle.

We Northwest natives just head out into the great, gloaming grey, and understand it is probably going to rain that day, and that we are going to get wet.

So be it.

Even back then, I understood that rain is pretty amazing: it's water coming down from the sky!

We don't expect this: we're used to the sky being just air, having no substance.

And then it starts raining, and where I live now, in Oregon—yet another rainy place in the Northwest—it can rain for a whole day, or days, without stopping. Water, just coming down from the sky.

As if the Universe is washing us clean.

There's this tendency to hole up when it rains; to concentrate on staying dry, on putting umbrellas up in defense.

But, in my experience, when it's raining the best thing to do is get outside and get wet, like the nature all around you.

Just go stand out there in your shirtsleeves, and let it happen. Face upturned, water pouring down, let the rain soak you through and through. Participate fully in this magical and mystical event that is happening to you right here, right now.

We think we're separate from this need to soak up water; we think because we're humans and don't have leaves or roots, we don't need it.

But we do.

We need to feel connected to our natural selves. We need to feel ourselves as part of the cosmos. We need to get washed clean by the Universe, just as much as anything on the planet.

Probably more.

PART ELEVEN

Becoming the Beloved

The Face of the Beloved

The face of the Beloved is the most beautiful face you've seen.

Other faces will appear beautiful, comely, pleasing to you.

But the face of the Beloved is loved beyond measure. You will recognize it instantly, and you will take this face in your hands and caress it as you might the face of your newborn babe.

Everything about the Beloved is reverent to you: the curve of their arm, the swell of their shoulder, each wrinkle and flaw and imperfection. This is love, the loving of another as much as yourself, with the same desire for preservation as you hold for yourself.

The body of the Beloved is like sweet oil—you want to rub it into your skin, a fragrant unguent that you cannot have too much of. Satiated with your Beloved, even then you desire more. This closeness is attainable only through God, this is where you and your Beloved will meet.

You may love many times. But this one love, this Beloved? This is the one that you will love most truly and deeply, you will feel them as a presence even when you are apart, you will speak to them with your mind even from a distance, you will call and your love will hear you, even from miles away.

The years spent in discovering your Beloved are not wasted. They are the journey to prepare you. Without these years, your heart is not opened enough to expand to this space with God, the three of you—the Beloved, you, God—all in a cloud of golden haze above your head.

It is a wonder, this gift of love.

Accept it, if it comes to you. Reach out your hand, untie the ribbon, pull away the wrapping paper, and stare in dazzling gratitude at your Beloved's beautiful, cherished face.

This Beloved is God/Universe/All/One.

This Beloved is also you.

Chaos Means Change

We speak of Flow as easy, effortless, what's happening now, what's simplest for you to move in.

We give you these markers: ease, joy, feeling right, to help you understand what Flow feels like, so you can recognize and use those feelings to gauge whether you are moving in this energy stream or need to adjust your efforts or your thoughts to get back into the stream.

Again, to be in Flow is to be doing what feels good in your soul Self. What is effortless, what seems to happen on its own, what is your heart's desire, what makes your soul sing, what your heart longs for at the deepest level.

In all these ways your heart and soul move you on your path of destiny, on your path of experiences that open and delight and bring you joy. This path of Flow may start out being guided by big goals, such as "I will make this much money" or "I will have this level of business" or "I will lose this much weight" or "I will create this particular level of success," or whatever it is for you.

Of course, these goals arrive to you out of the mood and flavor of the dominant culture: the need to be bigger, better, best, top, and so forth.

As if being smaller, lower, less might provide any less joy, any less value.

You do not have to be the "best" to be worthy, to be valid, to have the experiences you need to grow!

Dominant culture sets a trap, by this worship of success. We say, don't go into the trap. Understand yourself as soul first, here for experiences of beauty, joy, and connection. Let go of the desire for markers that don't mean anything.

Can you feel success in your heart?
Does being the best make you happier at a soul level?
Will more money create a better relationship for you?
Will more success give you the time you need for love?
And so forth.

You have heard both so often: the demand of the dominant culture to be better, bigger, best, and the cry of the alternative culture to slow down, go smaller, and more sustainable.

But as a soul in human form, you exist with a certain amount of time and energy in your human field. This means you can't do everything, all the time.

Choosing one thing means not choosing another. And so it is important to choose wisely, so you choose what is meaningful to your soul.

In certain cases, success on paper may be what is most meaningful. But for most of you, in this lifetime, success is not important. The experiences of love, connection, beauty, grace . . . these are all that matter.

Again, when you see things arriving effortlessly and easily, follow them. These are markers of Flow.

Conversely, when you see things are difficult, stuck, falling away, or moving into a state of chaos and confusion, trust that you are being guided, moved, nudged, and adjusted into a new position, so that you will have greater understanding. Often, chaos is what is needed when we have nudged you so many times into what is easy and effortless, and you have resisted!

You have been shown the path of Flow over and over again, and yet for whatever reason, you have stayed stuck, resisting this direction.

You can only move as freely as your mind is free. You can only move in Flow when your heart is open to this reality. Thus, when you resist Flow and continue to resist Flow, after a certain point you will begin to experience chaos.

Chaos arrives to clear you, to bring change when you are unable to change for yourself, to point and nudge and move you into a new direction, even when you have been unwilling to move yourself in that way.

Chaos brings change. Often, when you have been stuck, numbed, and resistant to the call of your own heart for a long time, when you have let human ego be in charge instead of soul Self, change is what is required to move you toward opening.

When you are in the swirl of chaos in your life, allow that you are changing. Allow that you have missed or overlooked or ignored the many ways we have whispered to you of Flow, and now the energy is running faster and deeper, so that you cannot miss it.

Chaos brings change, and change is what you are. There is no time you are not growing: even unto the moment of death, you are growing.

And for soul Self, this growth is infinite and eternal.

In this way, you may trust when you are in chaos, that dark, swirling change that might seem like change for no reason, or change for reasons you don't understand, or change that doesn't make sense or came out of nowhere. Trust that this chaos is really the Universe asking you to grow even more.

Release all that you are not, and step into your true life.

To look at your Misbeliefs, and let them go.
To drop from dominant culture, and live as your true Self.

To release all that you are not, and step into your true life.
To let go of fear, anger, pain, and live from your soul.

What is the most effortless, easy thing you could do today? What if you just did that thing, and let go of the rest? Do you understand that the Universe is able to reach you more easily when you are in a state of Flow? Do you realize that Flow brings more Flow?

Pain as Stuckness

If you spend a lot of time feeling pain, you are stuck.

By this we do not mean physical pain, which can be a representation of stuckness, but which can also be a gateway to other lessons and other knowings.

By this we mean emotional and spiritual pain, which are based on your understanding and your consciousness.

To be in emotional pain is to believe you are not love.
To be in spiritual pain, is to believe you are separate from Source.

Both of these, Misbeliefs.

You may be empathic, open, conscious to the point where you feel the pain of another, you feel the pain of the world. You sense the pain of one, because you know yourself as One.

> *To be in spiritual pain, is to believe you are separate from Source.*

It is natural and real to feel the pain of the world. However, where you get stuck is by believing you have to take this pain, claim it, absorb it, and carry it.

You do not.

If you feel another's pain, you may see it, know it, recognize it. But each of you must walk your own path. You can't walk the path for someone else, even if this person is someone you love very much: partner, parent, child, sibling, friend.

You may want to help, you may think that you are helping by taking on their karmic load, but this is not how soul growth works.

Each must walk his or her own path; this is the only way greater understanding arrives. This is true even for the smallest of you, the youngest, the oldest, those in need, those whom you perceive as having more challenges or needing more help.

In truth, each is provided the challenges in accordance with his or her potential for understanding in this lifetime.

Do not try to understand, qualify, or compare, for while each of you is on the path, you are all at different places on your path: some just beginning, some far along.

Do not judge. Simply hold compassion for those in pain; love them, for they are in the chaos that moves them forward.

Observe your own nature, how you alternate from sometimes dipping back into pain and lower vibration, of feeling yourself not as love, as feeling yourself separate . . . and sometimes dipping forward into love, Light, and the understanding that all is well.

Have compassion for yourself, love yourself as we love you, and move forward on your path knowing that all is well, that you are growing, and that the Light will always guide you.

Finally, observe those who have learned how to move beyond suffering, beyond pain, and who have gained the understanding of what it is to live in love. Learn from them. Follow them a ways, if you desire. Remember yet again: it is your own path to walk, and you must walk it in your own way.

If you feel pain, know that pain is a marker of stuckness. Look again to the Light, and remember who you really are.

Take a moment, and review a particular pain you feel, whether from the past or that you are experiencing right now. As you review this pain, ask the Universe to show you the root or the deeper lesson that is there for you. Allow yourself to be open to all answers.

Fear as Stuckness

When you live in fear, or have feelings of fear, it is because you don't understand your true essence.

It is not about trust, or safety, or courage. It's about understanding your true self as soul Self, and knowing that, as soul Self, you are infinite, eternal, and love.

In this way, where is fear?
Fear is not possible in this view.

Light illuminates darkness.
Levity lifts gravity.

In human view, of course, when you become locked into a particular view from human experience, without remembering or recognizing soul, you often become afraid.

You are afraid of pain.

You are afraid of loss.

You are afraid of confusion.

You are afraid of chaos.

You are afraid of violence.

You are afraid of change.

You are afraid of the unknown.

Above all, you are afraid of darkness.

It is right to discern darkness, and to acknowledge darkness, for darkness is what exists in lower vibrations. It is a clouding of right view, a covering of right understanding.

Darkness seeks to obscure Light.

Darkness seeks to retain the illusion of separation.

And yes, we say darkness is tricky, seductive, silky: it calls to the ego, invites the ego into the small dark cave where it can hide and fume and create chaos to no end.

Darkness is the master of illusion.

Whereas, Light reveals all, illuminates every dark corner and recess of your life and your heart, and leads you forward in radiance.

You can spend your time in fear, but you don't need to.

The result, the outcome, your destiny continues, whether you huddle in the corner and hide, or simply open in grace to the experiences of this lifetime.

We say also, fear keeps you from walking on your path; it keeps you from moving forward. Fear holds you on the side of the road, paralyzed with the what-ifs of progression.

Yet your journey is to walk in the mystery!
It's why you're here.

Your journey is to change, grow, adapt, experience, enjoy, love . . . and to do this all without knowing what is ahead, without foreseeing every detail, every event, every happening.

> *This decision: to walk in fear or to walk in trust, this is always your choice.*

The mystery is the gift.

And this gift allows you to let go of the idea that you can control the details, plot the course, wrap up everything tightly. Instead, you let go of ego, and walk in the mystery, ever open to what is now.

Fear is stuckness, no growth, no change, numbing out, disassociation, pain, and loss.
It's hiding on the side of the road, afraid to step onto your path.

This decision: to walk in fear or to walk in trust, this is always your choice.

Try a little bit today, to let go of your fear. Just set it down at the side of the road, and walk without it for a while, and see how that feels to not carry that great, heavy, oppressive, limiting load.

The air is delicious, when you walk in the mystery!
There is so much to experience and enjoy while you are here.

It is okay to not know what is next.

Again, we say, this is part of the gift of your life: to not know,
and to walk forward into it anyway.

How does understanding that your destiny continues, help you
live without fear? How does understanding your infinite nature
as eternal soul, help you live without fear?

LESSON 64

Learning to Love

● ●

As you begin to live in this new way: to become conscious of everything, to become aware of the extraordinary beauty and richness of every single moment, to open to all the ways that the Universe is speaking to you, all the time, you begin to understand something more.

This awareness?
This opening into consciousness?
This ability to speak the language of the Universe?
This ability to ask for guidance, and to receive it in everything?
This is love. You have opened yourself into love.

Not only the love between humans, or the love of places and events and ideas, which you have known for a long time. But your ability to love this force that is far more expanded than you: this Divine/One/All/God, the ineffable energy of Oneness.

And you have learned how to communicate with that energy, by becoming one with the essence of That.

You have learned to love the ocean, the dance and pull of the endless waves.
You have learned to love the wind, the way it moves as lightness.
You have learned to love all animal form, all natural form.
You have learned to love all energies and entities, all relationships and understanding.
You have learned to love everything, all the time, in all ways.

And you have learned this by paying attention, by waiting in stillness, and by allowing yourself to become one of One, in your search for understanding.

What was simple: a desire to speak the language of the Universe, has resulted in a deeper relationship:

You have fallen in love with the Universe.
And of course, the Universe has always been in love with you.

This experience of love outside of human relationship—outside of the way we relate as personalities—is a great new thing for most of you.

You experience love simply as what is: you open your heart to the beauty and grace and extraordinary miracle of everyday, and you become One with what surrounds you.

You listen to the ocean, you feel it, you experience it with your heart.

And in this listening, you understand the ocean as love.
You listen to the wind, you feel it, you experience it as one of One.
And in this listening, you understand the wind as love.

As you have learned to become rapt with attention to the Universe, you understood that the Universe is your Beloved.

You have paid rapt attention to the Universe, so that you may speak this language of everything, of all that is. . . .

And with this attention, love is what happens.

To be aware, is to understand everything as love.
To be conscious, is to understand everything as love.
To be in the Now moment, is to understand everything as love, in this moment, right here, right now.

Because that's how it always is.

And when you reach a particular understanding: when you release all that is not you, and allow all that is you to embrace you and infuse you . . . you come to this understanding of your true Self.

To be aware, is to understand everything as love.

You were long familiar with love as the energy between personalities, love as romance, love as sentiment . . . the personal, cultural, familiar side of love.

When you began to learn the language of the Universe, what you were actually doing, is learning to be in love with everything.

You were learning to love everything, as your true Beloved.

Love the alpha, love the omega, love the small and the big, love as all time, all energy, all everything.

When you begin to see love in this way, nothing is hidden. All becomes transparent and transmuted into love, when you look with heart open.

Think back to a time when you were crazy in love with someone or something, and recall the heightened, almost dizzying awareness of that time. When was the last time you felt this way about someone, something? About everyone, everything?

LESSON 65

Learning to Be Loved

You took your attention off Misbeliefs and learned to pay attention to What Is.

You let go of distractions and learned to pay attention to what was happening right at the moment, right where you are.

Not tripping out in the personality.
Not getting hung up in the past.
Not trying to skip the Now and hurry up into the future.

You let go of the aspects of your personality that caused pain, or suffering, or shame, and you began to show up as your soul Self.

You watched and listened and waited for the Universe, the way a lover attends to the Beloved.

Sometimes you were busy, doing the demands of your earth life. But always at the back of your mind, you knew yourself as soul.

You saw that this lifetime, the past lifetimes, the future lifetimes, all of these have been and will be you, as soul, showing up in different personalities and bodies and situations, seeking your true Self.

And with this understanding, this gentle knowing accompanies you every day, in all your activities, you began to let your soul lead. You began to have experiences from soul Self, as interpreted through the human heart.

Recall: the heart is where the soul resides.

And in doing this . . . you became less distracted by all the thoughts and Misbeliefs and distractions and addictions that this human life presents.

You let go of all that; or at least, you began to remember to let go of all that, more and more and more.

You learned to simply be in what is: to see and hear and feel from soul. And in doing this, you learned to speak the language of the Universe: you learned to understand how the Universe is communicating with you at all times, in all ways. . . .

And in this noticing of all the beauty and grace and wonder, you learned to love, with your whole heart open. You learned to love this great expansive energy of everything.

You saw with eyes open.
Heard with your whole heart.
Felt everything all at once.

And in this way you understood love.

Your heart expanded with love for the Universe!

And now, in this new feeling, in this state of love that has come from paying attention to everything all at once, to really showing up and being there . . . this state of love, this blissful feeling of levity and grace and wonder and amazement, so that your heart is expanding outside of your chest, you realize something new. . . .

It's not just that you have learned to speak the language of the Universe.

It's not just that you have learned to love the Universe.

It's that the Universe is loving you back.

The Universe is sending you a constant stream of affection, grace, bliss, healing. . . . It is sending it to you even now, at the etheric level, at the cellular level, at the body level, at the level of the outer world.

> *The Universe is loving you back.*

The Universe is loving you back.

This is happening all ways, all times. There is no way to stop it or prevent it, or to fall or fail or mess up so you can't receive it.

The Universe is loving you back. It's just what this is: all energy, which is love, all the time, for everyone and everything.

When you learn to speak the language of the Universe, you learn to sense this love: the love emanating from you as awe; the love returning from the Universe in every moment forever.

All you need to do to receive this love is to allow it, to say yes, to open your whole heart not just in your own outpouring of emotion, but in sensing what is all around you, arriving to you at all times.

To love, and to be loved. This is the soul's purpose.

You can't stop the Universe from loving you, even if you try, because the essence of the Universe is love—and so are you. What if you let yourself sink into this Divine reality? What if you just said yes?

Becoming the Beloved

•◦

We return to the beginning, and we remind you: the gift of walking the path of the spiritual psychic is not that you learn psychic tricks.

The siddhis, the psychic tricks and techniques that astonish, charm, and manipulate are not important to your soul; they are less than meaningless, simply another distraction of ego.

The gift of walking the path of the spiritual psychic is that in your desire to learn these tricks, to have this special intuitive knowledge, something else happens entirely.

You learn to slow down.
You learn to listen.
You learn to see.
You learn to notice.
You learn to feel it all.

All of this slowing down, paying attention, becoming aware, opening to everything, all of this allows you to speak the language of the Universe, to have direct knowing of all that is.

And in this re-education of yourself, you learn to live from your soul. Your soul becomes the place you live from, instead of the human personality, ego, attachments, and so on.

All the fluff, drama, discord, distraction . . . it becomes meaningless to you, when you are communing with the Universe at this higher level; when you are speaking and living this language of Oneness.

We say also, when you learn to speak the language of the Universe, you find something else.

This language is love.
The Universe speaks to you in love.
You receive understanding and answers in love.
The Universe responds again in love.

It is love without end: you loving the Universe, the Universe loving back, you as the Beloved and the Universe as the Beloved become the same, not separate in any way.

You become the Beloved, which is what you have always been, and what you always will be. There is no way to separate yourself from Beloved/God/One/All/Divine.

Even when you resist, or reject, or block, or don't believe, or distract, or shun, the Universe remains as it is and can only be: love.

Thus, the Universe/God/One/All is loving you, whether you are loving back or not.

The Universe/God/One/All is loving you, whether you are allowing this love or not.

There is no time this love does not exist: to you, from you, to you again. This is the same for all beings, for all matter, for all everything, for all is One.

Thus, your entire soul journey is to learn to love and to be loved.

Not just in relationship with those in human form.

But in relationship to everything, all at once.

There is no greater purpose. There is no greater path.

There is just this understanding, which you have been opening to in past lifetimes, in this lifetime, in future lifetimes, in all the times that you have been existing, not as human but as energy and other expressions.

> *Your entire soul journey is to learn to love and to be loved.*

Thus, in all times, in all your experiences of Now, you have been learning to love.

There is no other lesson, save this.

You are learning to love; you are learning to become the Beloved.

The Beloved that is you loving the Universe.

The Beloved that is the Universe loving you back.

And so on, and so on, forever.

This is your soul path; to love, and to allow yourself to be loved back, by everything, all at once, always.

And in each lifetime, to remember this understanding earlier or later, in your own perfect timing. As love, loving, being loved.

You, learning to love everything.
Everything loving you back.
You becoming the Beloved.

We are here to love. Love is the language, love is the secret, love is the awakening, love is the enlightenment. There is no other answer. Just you, learning to love everything.

Dreaming Your Death

One night, I dreamt I died.

We have all heard the warnings about this: if you dream you die, you will really die in that moment, they say. If you dream you die, it means you're going to die soon, they say.

But that wasn't my experience.

I dreamt I died, and in my dream, I actually died, I really died, I completely died . . . and then . . . my soul looked around, and saw that it was all the same.

"I died!"

"I'm here!"

"I died!"

"It's all the same!"

The me that was my soul, the me that was my consciousness . . . it didn't go anywhere.

As I was floating away from my body, my soul was experiencing everything exactly as I do now when I am in a state of awareness.

There was no death.

The soul lives on.

In my dream, I immediately understood that the soul has no fear of death, because there is no death: the soul is not snuffed out, shut down; the soul does not cease to exist.

This is all myth and Misbelief.

Even the things that are hard for humans when someone we love dies: the grief, the longing, the loneliness . . . those don't exist for the person who transitions.

It's just love and gratitude, and this sense of the extraordinary beauty of this adventure we call life, and the understanding that it is a gift to experience everything.

I've had the dream, and I'm guessing many of you have had the dream, and if you've had the dream, well . . . you know it's true.

Consciousness remains.

Filled with love and always in gratitude, the soul lives on.

Acknowledgments

I am grateful to everyone who's helped me bring this book to light: Dr. Steve Koc, Annie Wilder, the wonderful folks at Beyond Words and Simon & Schuster: Richard and Michele Cohn, Judith Curr, Emily Han, Emily Einolander, Cindy Nickles, Emmalisa Sparrow Wood, Lindsay Easterbrooks-Brown, Jenefer Angell, Corinne Kalasky, Jill Duncan, Judy Oaks, and Sara Blum. I'm also thankful for the support of Penney Peirce, Madisyn Taylor, Dr. Steven Farmer, Ajayan Borys, Debra Lynne Katz, Jenai Lane, Servet Hasan, Jodi Livon, Danielle Rama Hoffman, Angela Holton, Cameron Steele, and Meryl Moss. Finally, to all you beautiful souls who've journeyed with me for so many years now—exploring, pioneering, and continually pressing forward on the path of soul growth. We are true soul family, and I appreciate you beyond bounds.

Additional Resources

Messages from the Divine Free Study Course

Would you like to study *Messages from the Divine* with your book club, spiritual group, or for your own spiritual growth? For a limited time, readers of *Messages from the Divine* are invited to participate in a free online course that facilitates working with the Lessons in the book at an even deeper level.

With a copy of the print book or eBook, you may reference the teachings while you're doing the coursework. There is absolutely no charge for this course; it is a gift to you from Sara.

For complete details about this limited offering to use with your book club, spiritual group, or for your own personal study as you work with *Messages from the Divine*, visit **www.sarawiseman.com**.

Sara Wiseman's past titles include:

Writing the Divine: How to Use Channeling for Soul Growth & Healing
The Intuitive Path: The Seeker's Guide to Spiritual Intuition
Your Psychic Child: How to Raise Intuitive and Spiritually Gifted Kids of All Ages
The Four Passages of the Heart: Moving from Pain into Love
Living a Life of Gratitude: Your Journey to Grace, Joy & Healing
Intuition, Cancer and Miracles: A Passage of Hope & Healing
Writing with the Muse: A Guide to Conscious Creativity

Sara Wiseman's bestselling online courses include:

The 33 Lessons (33 Days to Divine Awakening)

Be a Divine Conduit for Guides & Angels

Become a Spiritual Psychic in 28 Days

Manifest Miracles in 28 Days

Release Yourself from Family Karma

Heal Your Love & Relationship Karma

Overcoming Body Shame

A Year of Spiritual Awakening in Your Inbox

How to Hear What the Universe Is Saying

Moving from Stuck to Flow

Understand That You Are Enough

Open Yourself to Your Guides & Angels

Psychic Opening for Absolute Beginners

Learn the Practice of Channeled Writing

Access the Healing Powers of Past Lives

Call in Your Beloved with Ease

Get Rid of Your Anxiety for Good

Intuition, Cancer & Miracles

Writing with the Muse

To learn more about Sara's work, access hundreds of free podcasts and teachings, sign up for her *Daily Divine* blog, and find out about *Intuition University* coursework and training, visit **www.sarawiseman.com**

The corporate mission statement of Beyond Words Publishing is *Inspire to Integrity*. To learn about Beyond Words and their bestselling books, DVDs, and more, visit **www.beyondword.com**.

About the Author

Sara Wiseman is a visionary spiritual teacher and Nautilus Award–winning author who has taught tens of thousands of students worldwide via her books, courses, and trainings.

In 2000, Sara had a near-death experience that resulted in a sudden opening of consciousness: she experienced the energy of God as pure radiance. Her intuitive abilities, which had been latent since childhood, opened fully. Her spiritual understanding expanded, and she began to see "beyond the veil." In 2004, she began to receive spiritual teachings in meditation. These messages arrived as written works over a period of thirteen years, and form the basis of her spiritual teachings.

Sara is the founder of *Intuition University*, and hosts the award-winning podcasts *Ask Sara* and *Spiritual Psychic*, with over 2.1 million listeners. She also writes the award-winning *Daily Divine* blog, which offers free spiritual teachings delivered directly via email.

Sara lives with her family in the forests of Oregon.